How to Make the World
a Better Place

How to Make the World a Better Place

116 Ways You Can Make a Difference

Jeffrey Hollender
with *Linda Catling*

W. W. Norton & Company
New York   London

The text of this book is composed in 11/13 Baskerville
with the display set in Futura Condensed and Savage
Composition and manufacturing by the Haddon Craftsmen, Inc.
Book design by Susan Hood

Library of Congress Cataloging-in-Publication Data

Hollender, Jeffrey.
    How to make the world a better place : 116 ways you can make a
difference / Jeffrey Hollender and Linda Catling. —Rev. ed.
        p.   cm.

    1. Voluntarism—United States—Handbooks, manuals, etc.
    2. Social action—United States—Handbooks, manuals, etc.
    3. Quality of life—United States—Handbooks, manuals, etc.
    4. Environmental protection—United States—Handbooks, manuals,
    etc. I. Catling, Linda. II. Title.
    HN90.V64H65   1995
    361.2—dc20   94-43127

ISBN 0-393-31291-7

W. W. Norton & Company, Inc.
500 Fifth Avenue, New York, N.Y. 10110
W. W. Norton & Company Ltd.
10 Coptic Street, London WC1A 1PU

1 2 3 4 5 6 7 8 9 0

 This book is printed on recycled paper
using soy-based inks.

This book is dedicated to my mother, Lucille, who taught me how to care so much, and my new daughter Chiara for whom, like all of our children, it matters most.

—Jeffrey Hollender

This book is dedicated to Brad and Julie Catling, who have shown over and over again how two people can translate their hopes and aspirations for the world into actions that make a difference.

—Linda Catling

Contents

Contents

Contents

Contents

Contents

Contents

Acknowledgments

Because no book belongs to the authors alone, we want to acknowledge and thank everyone who joined us in creating this work: all the organizations mentioned on these pages whose dedication has greatly enriched the world and whose guidance and information have been invaluable to us; the many friends, colleagues, and family members who offered thoughtful suggestions and fresh ideas; Justin Chapman, Phil Girton, Orpheus Korshak, Oren Kronick, Linda Lyons, Judy McVickar, Jonathan Radigan, Laurie Shea, and Jeff Walker for their help with research and review of the manuscript; and Kerry Walker for infusing the book with her perspective and genuine caring, as well as putting in long hours at critical junctures.

Foreword: How to Put This Book into Action

The actions that make up this book can be read in any order you choose. You can start at the beginning and work your way through each of the eight sections or you can skip around, picking those actions that appeal to you most.

Each action is introduced with background information followed by a "What You Can Do" section that contains one or a series of specific actions. Don't get bogged down by all the introductory facts—if they seem overwhelming you can always skip ahead to the action. But if you like facts, figures, and some fairly amazing information, you'll find more than enough to meet your appetite in each introduction.

At the beginning of many sections, we've footnoted the sources we found particularly interesting or helpful. We have included them to give you more avenues to explore, as you discover the multitude of ways in which you can personally make the world a better place. For more information and additional resources in any of these areas, check out the wealth of information available in your local library, in the yellow pages, or from the university extension services in your area.

Introduction: The 5 Percent Solution

You're well acquainted with the problems. Descriptions of the world's woes blare from TV sets, fill endless pages of newsprint, are the focus of international symposia, and are studied, monitored, and evaluated by people in governments, universities, multinational corporations, and independent agencies. This book is not yet another description of what's gone wrong. It is, in the most basic, simple, and straightforward manner possible, about solutions to those problems and what you can do today to help make the solutions work.

Buckminster Fuller observed that by changing the minds of 5 percent of the population, one could effectively change the way society operates. Congratulations on being part of the 5 percent that's going to change the world . . . for the better! The actions you take today really *can* have an effect that will be felt far into the future. Consider for a moment the long-reaching effects of the women's suffrage movement, the civil rights movement, and the move to make our cities more accessible to the handicapped—all supported at first by just a small group of people like you who cared enough to do something. The mess we're in now was brought about by individuals acting in concert. It's individuals like you, all headed in the same direction, who can get us headed back in the right directions.

Grassroots action takes many forms. You may choose to be a vocal dissenter at public hearings on a proposed incinerator or a quiet consumer, using your buying power to support environmental action and social justice. In the pages that follow you'll learn about the hidden power in your shopping list and how to make some important connections with an ordinary computer. You'll learn how your rights as a citizen, shareholder, customer, or employee will bring presidents, politicians, and corporate executives to almost any bargaining table.

The simple actions contained in this book, grounded in solid information, can make the world a better place. When electronic mail messages were received by a head of state, political prisoners were set free. The toothpaste you use can support a company that selects women and minorities for positions of responsibility or one that encourages teenage addiction to tobacco and pollutes our rivers, streams, and lakes with dioxins. A dollar spent with a cooperative venture spreads the ethics of fair, responsible, and honest business in a marketplace full of inferior products manufactured by uncaring corporations.

We'll cover issues ranging from rebuilding community to hunger and homelessness, water pollution, corporate responsibility, and citizen diplomacy. You'll learn how to help build low-income housing, use recycled products, contribute to a food bank, invest money in a socially responsible manner, free prisoners of conscience, pass legislation through the U.S. Congress, and encourage world peace.

Have fun with the actions; choose the ones that really appeal to you. Do what you love and watch the world change! When you're done with this book, lend it to friends and coworkers. Copy particularly compelling sections and send them to your friends. The more people who understand how much power they have, the faster changes will take place.

Everything you need to step into action is included, from phone numbers and addresses to names, titles, background statistics, and quotable information. Each action is designed to generate the greatest impact in the least amount of time. Results are guaranteed without your having to quit your job or give away your life savings.

How to Make the World
a Better Place

Part I

Building Community

How you can start to make the world a better place right in your own backyard by connecting with neighbors, improving community economics, saving open spaces, and having fun doing it

Chapter 1

In Your Own Backyard

In her book *The Wagon and the Star: A Study of American Community Initiative*, Margaret Mead describes the 1950s radio broadcasts entitled *The People Act* as one of radio's greatest achievements. "These broadcasts were vivid descriptions of activities initiated and carried out by citizens to solve community problems or to enrich community life. The response from listeners was so overwhelming that the broadcasters had to employ a staff to answer inquiries about ways in which communities could start cooperative actions or solve problems of community organization."

Behind *The People Act* was Elmore McKee, a dedicated member of the American Friends Service Committee, who had gone to Germany at the close of World War II to help ignite a spark in the country's devastated communities. As Mead tells it, "He saw at close range the crushing human effect of twelve years of Nazi dictatorship. In postwar Germany, he found no community spirit; individual initiative had been so harshly repressed for so long that people were afraid to think for themselves and gladly left all community decision-making to public authorities."

For the first time, McKee fully realized how easily people can lose the right to govern themselves. Could the United States, he wondered, lose its independence through carelessness?

When we contemplate the future of this country, it is our own apathy we should fear, not the magnitude of the problems we face. The building blocks of community life—extended families, social clubs, religious organizations, and the like—are in decline because we have turned our collective attention elsewhere. What better time than now to rediscover the power that comes from paying attention to what's going on in our own backyards?

To those who ask "What can I do? I'm just one among thousands," the answer is "A lot." In 1990 the people of Hoboken, New Jersey, learned a lesson about participation they will not soon forget. Town residents got to witness the power of the individual firsthand when they forced the local government to hold a public referendum to decide the future of their waterfront. A mere twelve votes saved the town from massive development that would have eliminated views and severely limited public access.

Voting is just one way to make a difference in your community. There are as many positive actions as there are community members. The key is to feel committed enough to care what happens, and that starts with feeling connected to the people and institutions around you. Problems as wide-ranging as crime, mental health, and environmental degradation can be helped only by our strengthening the bonds between individuals and creating caring communities that foster those bonds. The following sections offer traditional and innovative ideas for getting more connected to the place you call home.

Chapter 2

Building Your Own Community

Building community can be as simple as getting together with like-minded individuals to hash over the events of the week, discuss a new book, or enjoy a spirited game of charades.

Action!
Join Your Neighborhood *Utne* Salon

The aroma of coffee and muffins wafts through the air. A loose circle of well-worn, comfortable chairs, each a different design, has been assembled for the dozen or so participants now stirring in them. The ensuing two-hour salon/discussion/debate/gab session transmutes into something transcendent—conversation-

Sources for this section include: Paul Glover, "The Ultimate Barter," *Mother Earth News,* Aug./Sept. 1993; "What You Can Do," *Co-op America Quarterly,* Summer 1994 (for more information about Co-op America, see Action 61); Jan Marie Werblin, "The Kindness Revolution," *Changes,* June 1994 (Deerfield Beach, FL); Gary Snyder, "Not Here Yet," *Shambhala Sun,* March 1994 (Boulder, CO); Gary Snyder, "Want a Tribe? Stay Put," *Utne Reader,* July/ Aug. 1992 (Minneapolis, MN).

al and conceptual jazz. One person's ideas inspire another's, and another's. Each contributes his or her own piece to something larger. By making explicit what may have been, prior to the salon, only flickering at the edges of their own awareness, they enrich and elevate the level of discourse among themselves and, by extension, in society as a whole.

Historically, literary salons (the word *salon* is French for living room) have been hotbeds of intellectual activity where brilliant authors and philosophers would gather to present their latest work, to meet patrons and other influential folk, and just to do some freestyle scintillation. It has been said of French history that the aristocratic ladies of the salons were the midwives of the Enlightenment.

The present-day "midwife of the Enlightenment" for hundreds of groups around the country is the *Utne Reader*'s Neighborhood Salon Association. Brainchild of the magazine that has dubbed itself "the best of the alternative press," the association exists for the purpose of bringing together like-minded individuals interested in discussing everything from literature and philosophy to politics and social reform. Each group is autonomous and sets its own agenda; the association serves as a matchmaker, introducing prospective members to existing groups and helping those who want to form new groups.

Today salons are being held all over America. In apartment living rooms and suburban church basements, in coffee shops and pubs and parks, friends and neighbors are coming together to engage in very un-small talk. They're cultivating their powers of creativity and reviving the endangered art of conversation. Salons may be the antidote to the atomized and media-saturated lifestyle that prevails in premillennial America. Their proliferation is integral to the search for community, citizenship, and purpose in a society gone haywire on materialism and individual achievement.

We need to get together and talk with one another about the things we care about and believe in. It's fun. It's hip. And it can change the world.

What You Can Do

To join the Neighborhood Salon Association, send $12 to: Neighborhood Salon Association, c/o *Utne Reader*, 1624 Harmon Place, Minneapolis, MN 55403, or call (612) 338-5040. A lifetime membership includes: a list of people nearby who want to get together, including contact information on any existing salons in your area; a copy of *Salon-keeper's Companion: Guide to Conducting Salons, Councils, and Study Circles;* access to *Utne*'s national salon directory; and placement in an Internet E-mail salon.

Action 2

Do What You Love and Community Will Follow

In 1994 the Burlington, Vermont, arts community got a taste of how powerful strong community can be and how responsive it can be in time of need.

One night in early spring, fire ravaged the house of three young artists, destroying their possessions, including all but a few pieces of their art. Less than a week later, Burlington Arts was organizing a fund-raising auction. It had collected donations from almost every artist in town and found an appropriate space, an auctioneer, and numerous volunteers. This spontaneous art auction drew over two hundred people and raised close to $9,000 to help the fire victims.

What You Can Do

Whatever your passion, you can be sure there are people out there who'd love to have you join them. Start a reading group or join an *Utne* salon (see Action 1). Join your area arts council or hiking club. Bulletin boards—at your local food co-op, natural foods store, grocery store, community college or university, Laundromat, outdoor gear store—are great places to post notices and to read other people's notices. Or place a personal ad, looking for like-minded individuals with whom to share your interests. The following organizations can put you in touch with local chapters of groups near you:

To learn more about museum volunteers in the United States, contact:

American Association of Museums
1225 Eye St., NW
Suite 200
Washington, DC 20005
(202) 289-1818

To find out more about National Arts and Humanities Month or the location of an arts agency near you, contact:

The National Assembly of Local Arts Agencies
927 15th St., NW
12th Floor
Washington, DC 20005
(202) 371-2830

The National Assembly of State Arts Agencies
1010 Vermont Ave., NW
Suite 920
Washington, DC 20005
(202) 347-6352

If you are interested in planting trees in your community, contact Tree People, a community-based, nonprofit, environmental organization dedicated to showing citizens how to plant and care for trees. It runs environmental leadership programs for tens of thousands of children each year and provides tree-planting advice and technical training to community groups and interested individuals. Its Citizen Forester Training program publishes a very informative book entitled *The Simple Act of Planting a Tree*. Contact the group at:

Tree People
12601 Mulholland Dr.
Beverly Hills, CA 90210
(818) 753-4600

If you are interested in getting your feet wet while helping to protect local rivers in your area, contact the River Network. It can provide you with information on national projects as well as refer you to projects in your area.

River Network
P.O. Box 8787
Portland, OR 97207-8787
Telephone: (800) 423-6747 or (503) 241-3506
Fax: (503) 241-9256
E-mail: rivernet@igc.apc.org

If you are more interested in protecting wildlife, contact one of the five hundred national wildlife refuges in the United States. Volunteer to maintain the habitats and refuge facilities, feed and care for animals, photograph natural areas, conduct research, help with archaeological and biological projects, lead tours, conduct surveys, or help with public outreach. To find out about opportunities in your area, contact the volunteer coordinator at your regional U.S. Fish and Wildlife Service office:

- ✔ Alaska Region: 1011 E. Tudor Rd., Anchorage, AK 99503; (907) 786-3391
- ✔ North Atlantic Region (Connecticut, Delaware, Maine, Maryland, Massachusetts, New Hampshire, New Jersey, New York, Pennsylvania, Rhode Island, Vermont, Virginia, and West Virginia): 300 Westgate Center Dr., Hadley, MA 01035; (413) 253-8200
- ✔ Northern Region (Illinois, Indiana, Iowa, Michigan, Minnesota, Missouri, Ohio, and Wisconsin): 1 Federal Dr., Federal Bldg., Fort Snelling, MN 55111; (612) 725-3691

- ✔ Pacific Region (California, Hawaii, Idaho, Nevada, Oregon, and Washington): 911 NE 11th Ave., Eastside Federal Complex, Portland, OR 97232-4181; (503) 231-6173
- ✔ Rocky Mountain Region (Colorado, Kansas, Montana, Nebraska, North Dakota, South Dakota, Utah, and Wyoming): Denver Federal Center, Box 25486, Denver, CO 80225; (303) 236-8148
- ✔ Southern Region (Alabama, Arkansas, Florida, Georgia, Kentucky, Louisiana, Mississippi, North Carolina, South Carolina, and Tennessee): 1875 Century Blvd., Atlanta, GA 30349; (404) 679-7187
- ✔ Southwest Region (Arizona, New Mexico, Oklahoma, and Texas): P.O. Box 1306, Albuquerque, NM 87103; (505) 766-8044

Action 3

Community Gardens

Community gardens are a wonderful way to save money and lower your impact on the planet by growing your own produce. They are also a wonderful way to meet people and build community spirit.

Community gardens have been popular in the United States since the turn of the century. One recently took shape across the Hudson River from Manhattan, in Hoboken, New Jersey, on the former site of several condemned buildings.

The garden officially opened on April 22, Earth Day 1994, with the picking of plots and the laborious task of clearing bricks and rubble from the site. As the morning wore on and only a third of the plots had been claimed, organizers began to worry that the project would flop. But their fears were unfounded; by noon aspiring gardeners had claimed 90 percent of the plots. Neighborhood residents who didn't sign up for gardening space contributed buckets of water, entertained gardeners with salsa music, and picked up trash along the street.

Located in a predominantly low-income, Hispanic neighborhood, the garden draws an ethnically diverse group, ranging in ages from three to ninety and coming from a wide range of economic backgrounds. "Most of us are here to garden and enjoy each other's company," says one participant, "but there are some people who come just to have fun and to feel like part of something special."

What You Can Do

To find out more about community gardens in your area or to get tips about starting one, contact the American Community Gardening Association at 325 Walnut St., Philadelphia, PA 19106. The association has local branches in every state and publishes *Community Greening Review* magazine.

Action 4
Bartering

The most ancient form of economic exchange, bartering, is enjoying a renaissance in the United States. Along with providing economic benefits, bartering is helping build community spirit among friends and neighbors and even in an entire town.

In New York City members of a group called Womanshare exchange their time and talent for services they might not otherwise be able to afford. Here's how it works: in exchange for an hour of labor, be it massage, carpentry, or child care, members receive an hour of credit that can be used to buy services from anyone in the group. Begun in 1992 by a few underemployed friends who agreed to barter services among themselves, Womanshare currently numbers seventy strong, with many more women on the waiting list.

Farther north, in Ithaca, New York, bartering has become a way of life for many. The system in Ithaca, known as Ithaca HOURS, was begun by Paul Glover and other local residents to stem the tide of dollars leaving the community and to help eliminate the wage disparity that exists there. The Ithaca system works on the same principle as Womanshare: for every hour of

13

labor that participants contribute, they earn an hour of credit. The group boasts over eight hundred members and has issued more than $44,000 worth of currency, called Ithaca HOURS. HOURS can be used in exchange for a wide variety of goods and services, ranging from produce at the farmers' market to meals at local restaurants. Even movies, eye exams, and dental checkups can be purchased with HOURS.

What You Can Do

Bartering can be as simple or as elaborate as you want to make it. Test the waters by trading your gourmet cooking skills for the use of a friend's boat, or agree to help a friend paint her house in exchange for help planting your garden.

If you'd like to explore bartering possibilities in more detail, send $1.50 to *Co-op America Quarterly*, c/o Co-op America, 1850 M St., NW, #700, Washington, DC 20036, for a packet of information on Womanshare and other work exchanges.

If you're really ambitious, send $25 for Paul Glover's *Hometown Money Starter Kit*, which includes forms, laws, barter articles, past issues of *Ithaca Money*, samples of Ithaca HOURS, photocopies of depression-era scrip from your city or state, and more. Write to *Ithaca Money*, Box 6578, Ithaca, NY 14851.

Action 5
The Co-oping of America

Belonging to a buying club or a co-op is a great way to get together with friends, neighbors, or complete strangers and help your pocketbook at the same time. Many communities have established food co-ops that you can join for nominal fees. Many co-ops utilize the volunteer labor of their members, so you may need to pitch in and help a few hours a month. Most communities also have buying clubs made up of individuals who place orders together from a wholesaler. Members usually take turns organizing the buys and separating orders when the shipments come in.

What You Can Do

Join your local food co-op or start one yourself. The National Cooperative Business Association, 1401 New York Ave., NW, Suite 1100, Washington, DC 20005; (800) 636-6222, has a free information package to help you. It includes information on starting a club and a list of wholesalers who supply clubs (these wholesalers can also let you know about existing clubs in your area).

Action 6

Random Acts of Kindness

A woman in San Francisco recently created a stir when she paid bridge tolls for herself—and the six cars behind her. A news report on the incident was followed by a rash of people pumping money into the expired parking meters of complete strangers.

Despite the grim news reports of unkind acts people continue to perpetrate on one another, there seems to be a quiet revolution going on in this country. An increasing number of people have decided that being nice has its own rewards. When did the revolution start? Hard to say, but it got its bumper-sticker slogan in the early 1980s, when Anne Herbert jotted the words "Practice random kindness and senseless acts of beauty" on a placemat in a San Francisco diner. The phrase moved around the country as informal graffiti for years before it made its way into the mainstream.

What You Can Do

If in the course of your busy day you've forgotten all the pleasantries you learned as a child, don't despair. There are a number of wonderful books out now that will remind you not only of the myriad ways to be nice, but just how good it feels to make someone else's day.

Why not:

✔ Smile at someone you don't know
✔ Thank your mailperson
✔ Give someone a hug
✔ Tell someone you love him or her
✔ Put some change in an expired parking meter
✔ Pay someone a genuine compliment
✔ Write a card to someone you haven't seen in a while
✔ Call your oldest friend
✔ List the birthdays of everyone you know, post the list on your refrigerator—then send a card or phone each one on the birthday
✔ Let someone pull in front of you in heavy traffic
✔ Listen to a child
✔ Pay the toll for the car behind you
✔ Give the person in front of you at the checkout a little money if he or she is short of cash
✔ Help someone carry groceries to the car
✔ Give a parent a break—watch his or her child for an hour

For more great ideas, look at these books:

Acts of Kindness, by Hancock and Meladee McCarthy (Deerfield Beach, FL: Health Communications, Inc., 1994)
Chicken Soup for the Soul, by Mark Victor (Deerfield Beach, FL: Health Communications, Inc., 1993)
Guerrilla Kindness, by Gavin Whitsett (Manassas Park, VA: Impact Publishers, 1994)
Random Acts of Kindness (Emeryville, CA: Conari Press, 1994)

Action 7
Volunteering to Build Community

A few summers ago 120 people volunteered their time to help rebuild Detroit neighborhoods through the Detroit Summer program. Ex-gang members worked side by side with college students and other young adults from around the country, restoring vacant houses, planting trees, painting senior citizens' houses, turning abandoned lots into parks, and painting murals. This burst of energy at the grassroots level changed the faces of many communities and enhanced the lives of the people who live there.

Detroit Summer (see Action 68) is just one of a thousand different ways in which volunteers can build community. Literacy programs, museums, AIDS hospices, libraries, and homeless shelters all depend on community volunteers. No effort is too large or too small when it comes to offering your time as a volunteer.

What You Can Do

1. If you are looking for inspiration or are just interested in what other individuals are doing to make the world a better place, check out a new magazine called *Who Cares,* which fills each issue with heartwarming success stories of volunteer activism in the United States. Send $15 for a quarterly subscription to *Who Cares,* 1511 K St., NW, Suite 1042, Washington, DC 20005; (202) 628-1691.

2. If you have time to donate and want to find an organization that really needs you, call Ecoline, a joint project of the Together Foundation for Global Community and the University of Vermont. Ecoline will be happy to put you in touch with an organization in your area that needs help. Call (800) 326-5463.

   Below is a sampling of national volunteer organizations that will gladly put you in touch with local chapters that need your help. You will find throughout this book the names and addresses of other great volunteer organizations that could use your help, or consult *Volunteer USA* by Andrew Carroll (New York: Fawcett, 1991) or *Golden Opportunities: A Volunteer Guide for Americans over 50,* Andrew Carroll (Petersons Guides, 1994).

Literacy Hotline
Sega Services
P.O. Box 81826
Lincoln, NE 68501
(800) 228-8813
Call to find out how you can get involved with literacy programs in your area.

National AIDS Hotline
American Social Health Association
P.O. Box 13827
Research Triangle Park, NC 27709
(800) 342-AIDS
Call to find out how you can volunteer to staff a hotline in your area.

The National Committee for the Prevention of Child Abuse
(NCPCA)
332 S. Michigan Ave.
Suite 1600
Chicago, IL 60604-4357
(312) 663-3520

Special Olympics
1350 New York Ave., NW
Suite 500
Washington, DC 20005
(202) 628-3630
Call to find out how you can help mentally challenged children and adults train to compete in a variety of Olympic-type sports.

The Sunshine Foundation
2001 Bridge St.
Philadelphia, PA 19124
(800) 767-1976 or (215) 535-1413
The Sunshine Foundation is a national organization that is dedicated to answering the dreams and wishes of chronically and terminally ill chil-

dren (ages 3–21). There are thirty chapters nationwide, all of them staffed by volunteers.

Volunteers of America
3813 North Causeway Blvd.
Metairie, LA 70002
(504) 837-2652
Call for the number of the local office nearest you. It will put you in touch with volunteer opportunities in your area.

Action 8
Volunteers in Service to Uncle Sam

The Clinton administration has made a strong commitment to community building that's providing a wide variety of volunteer opportunities for all ages. The Corporation for National and Community Service offers full- and part-time volunteer and stipend positions. Here are some of the volunteer opportunities it offers.

Civilian Community Corps (CCC)
In 1994–95 more than one thousand young people will serve in the new Civilian Community Corps. The CCC is a national residential service option in which participants are housed and trained together on military bases and deployed as teams to community service sites. The corps provides participants with opportunities to meet real community needs as well as to develop their own leadership skills and receive invaluable training for future careers.

Volunteers in Service to America (VISTA)
VISTA is a full-time, year-long program for men and women age 18 or older who commit themselves to increasing the capabilities of low-income people to improve the conditions of their own lives. VISTA volunteers serve in rural and urban areas, sharing their skills and experience in fields such as employment

training, literacy, shelter for the homeless, and neighborhood revitalization.

Learn and Serve America Programs

These school-based programs integrate service into daily academic life. The young people participate actively in service experiences that meet community needs and foster a lifetime commitment to service.

The **K–12 Program** supports school- and community-based organizations that engage school-aged youth in service. Over 275,000 students in all fifty states participate in service activities that are integrated into their curricula, providing structured time for service and time for the students to think, talk, or write about their service experiences.

Higher Education Innovation Programs engage college students in meeting pressing community needs. Higher education projects support high-quality community service and service-learning initiatives at colleges and universities across the nation. Some are student-run; some are faculty-led; many are integrated with academic study. As essential parts of the college experience, these efforts will create a new generation of leaders committed to service.

National Senior Service Corps (NSSC)

The NSSC utilizes the skills, talents, and experience of older Americans in addressing urgent issues facing the nation. Together these programs involve over 470,000 volunteers who serve 1,223 local projects and devote an annual total of over 111 million hours of service to their local communities.

The **Foster Grandparent Program** offers low-income persons age 60 and over the opportunity to serve one-on-one with children and young people who have special needs, including teen parents and children who are abused and neglected. Over 23,000 foster grandparents serve twenty hours a week in such volunteer stations as hospitals, public schools, day care centers, and correctional institutions.

Senior Companion Program volunteers are low-income men and women age 60 and over. Senior companions provide individual support and assistance to other adults, primarily the homebound elderly. Their services help the homebound achieve and maintain their highest level of independent living. Approximately 13,000 senior companions provide disability assistance, home management assistance, and social and recreational companionship to approximately 32,000 individuals each year.

The **Retired and Senior Volunteer Program (RSVP)** is a network of 430,000 Americans, age 55 and up, who perform a wide range of volunteer services that meet community needs and effectively use their skills, interests, and experience. RSVP provides communities with volunteers diverse in experience, interest, income, and education, who are ready to take on the challenges facing the country.

What You Can Do

To learn more about any of these programs, contact the Corporation for National Service, 1100 Vermont Ave., NW, Washington, DC 20525. Telephone: (202) 606-5000; fax: (202) 606-4854.

Action 9
Running for Office

Getting involved in grassroots politics is no small undertaking, but it is one of the best ways to help shape the future of the place you live and to help prevent some of the developmental disasters wrought by local politicians in too many communities. Some positions require a full-time commitment, but many grassroots politicians do important work part-time, in addition to their full-time jobs. Here are just some of the many elected positions that need to be filled by citizens like you:

Planning commission member
Treasurer

Zoning board member
School board member
Housing review board member
City clerk
Constable
Library board member
County clerk
Sergeant-at-arms

The task can be immense, but so can the rewards: a real sense of empowerment, the ability to empower others, and the ability to make or influence good decisions. Every election is important. If you can get involved, do so!

What You Can Do

At the heart of democracy is the voting booth. If you do nothing else, make sure you show up on election day to support candidates who share your views.

If you are interested in running for office or just learning more about grassroots politics and community activism, *The Sierra Club Guide to Community Organizing: How to Save Your Neighborhood, City, or Town,* by Maritza Pick (San Francisco: Sierra Club Books, 1993), and *Quickening of America,* by Frances Moore Lappé and Paul Martin DuBois (San Francisco: Jossey-Bass, 1994) are great resources.

Action 10
Staying Put

According to poet and ecologist Gary Snyder, we are a nation of homeless people because so few of us stay put long enough to feel a sense of obligation and commitment or to take a serious interest in local politics and the workings of our communities. He quotes Daniel Kemmis, who served as mayor of Missoula, Montana: "What holds people together long enough to discover their power as citizens is their common inhabiting of a single place." Snyder himself puts it this way: "A commitment to place is not just good environmentalism, not just a move towards resolving social and economic problems, but also a means for us to become citizens in both the natural and the social worlds. If the ground can be our common ground, we can begin to talk to one another once again."

There is a powerful argument to be made for finding a place we really want to be and for committing ourselves to it. For some people that means staying where they are or striking out to find the perfect neighborhood; for others it means creating an entirely new place, as is evidenced by the growing number of "intentional communities." The key is finding a place you can call your own—and then staying put.

What You Can Do

Even if you don't know how long you'll be in your current neighborhood, act as if you're there for life. Make a commitment to get to know your local politicians, local business owners, and your neighbors, as well as your local flora and fauna. Take an interest in what happens in your community.

If you're contemplating a move, you might consider joining a cohousing or other intentional community or even starting one of your own. A couple of good references are *Cohousing: A Contemporary Approach to Housing Ourselves,* by Kathryn McCamant and Charles Durrett (Berkeley: Habitat Press/Ten Speed Press) and the *Directory of Intentional Communities* (available from Community Service Books, P.O. Box 243, Yellow Springs, OH 45387; (513) 767-2161).

Chapter 3

Parks and Open Spaces

P arks, recreation areas, and open spaces are seen by many, particularly politicians, as pleasant "frills"; not surprisingly, budgets for public green spaces are often the first to be cut in hard economic times. But the fact is, these special places are essential to our physical and spiritual health, not to mention the health of our communities.

It takes four mature trees to replace the oxygen that each of us breathes. As more and more land is covered over with concrete, where will these trees live if not in urban parks? In the past few decades, Americans have fled the cities to seek a higher quality of life in suburban and rural areas. But the result has been new cities springing up in these outlying areas. Current trends indicate that by the end of the twentieth century 80 percent of us will be living in urban areas. The livability of our cities will depend a great deal on the quantity and quality of green open spaces that are available to everyone.

According to New York City's Neighborhood Open Space Coalition, when Central Park was completed in 1873 the value of surrounding properties increased so dramatically that the city generated an addition $4 million in tax revenue. Recent studies have found that simply planting trees on a city street increases

Sources for this section include "Stop Overs," *EcoTraveler*, March/April 1994.

the value of adjacent houses by approximately 6 percent. And the 1989 Halstead Real Estate Report noted that apartments with a good park or river view were valued up to 20 percent higher than those which did not. In light of such statistics, how could any city say parks are a luxury it can't afford?

Urban green spaces absorb storm water, remove pollution from the air, and reduce city noise. They also affect city life. According to the Trust for Public Lands, "As early as 1967, the National Advisory Commission on Civil Disorders, in reporting on the causes of rioting that swept many American cities that summer, stated: 'Grievances concerning municipal recreation programs were found in a large majority of the 20 cities and appeared to be one of the most serious complaints in half.' More recently, residents of the four areas most affected by the 1992 civil disorder in Los Angeles saw youth services and parks as the most pressing needs in their neighborhoods."

Action 11

Lobbying for Open Spaces

Although there is growing grassroots support for parks and open spaces, this support is not reflected in city budgets. More parks are needed in most cities and existing parks are in dire need of better maintenance.

What You Can Do

Let your state and local representatives know that you feel strongly about the need for maintaining and expanding the park system in your city. For more information, contact the Trust for Public Land, 116 New Montgomery, 4th Floor, San Francisco, CA 94105.

Action 12

Marching for Parks

Every year communities across the country, with the help of corporate sponsors, raise millions of dollars to fund new playgrounds, park cleanups, and educational materials. The annual March for Parks is organized by the National Parks and Conservation Association (NPCA), a nonprofit citizens' group dedicated to preserving national parks; 100 percent of the money raised by the event goes toward enhancing local parks and recreation areas.

What You Can Do

To learn more about March for Parks, contact NPCA at (202) 223-6722.

Action 13

Rails-to-Trails Conservancy

When the great railroads laid their tracks across the country, little did they know they would help to preserve prime open spaces for later generations.

Many of the railroads have faded into history, and the tracks the trains once thundered over are rusty and overgrown, but thanks to an organization called Rail-to-Trails Conservancy, thousands of miles of unused track are being converted to urban, suburban, and rural bike paths and multiuse trails.

Railroad rights-of-way, which are often 50 to 100 feet wide, make perfect recreational pathways for bicyclists, in-line skaters, walkers, joggers, birdwatchers, and cross-country skiers. Some of the newly converted trails are perfect for commuters and schoolchildren, who can now safely walk or ride bikes to schools, offices, or subway stations. One trail in northern Virginia is 44 miles long and has over two million users a year.

Since 1986, Rails-to-Trails has helped local communities convert more than 7,000 miles of abandoned rail corridors into recreation ways. The number of rail trails has jumped from fewer than 100 to over 600, with an additional 650 projects under way nationwide. The mission of Rails-to-Trails is twofold: not only is the group working to expand the urban trail system in the United States, but members also hope that by saving existing rights-of-way from development, the corridors may one day be converted for use by light-rail commuter trains that could help relieve our dependence on cars.

What You Can Do

If there is an unused section of railroad track in your community, contact Rails-to-Trails. It is experienced in helping ordinary citizens go through every step of the process to turn unused track into a multiuse trail.

Rails-to-Trails Conservancy
1400 16th St., NW
Suite 300
Washington, DC 20036
(202) 797-5400

Chapter 4

Helping the Homeless

The first step to giving much-needed help to homeless individuals and families in your area is to realize that the age-old stereotypes concerning the homeless are generally untrue.

Many believe that people who are homeless are unemployed and homeless by choice. This is far from the truth. Less than 6 percent of the people living on America's streets have chosen to be homeless. Many of our homeless are minimum-wage earners who can't support their families or afford to pay rent in the inner cities. The homeless are often labeled heavy drug users and seen as dangerous. Research suggests that only one in four homeless people is a substance abuser and that, although tragic encounters do occur, the homeless are among the least threatening groups in our society. They are more often the victims of crime than the perpetrators.

Sources for this section include: *Fifty-four Ways You Can Help the Homeless,* by Rabbi Charles A. Kroloff (Southport, CT: Hugh Lauter Levin, Assoc., 1993).

Action 14

Respect the Dignity of All People

What You Can Do

Homeless people not only lack shelter, but are treated as if they don't exist. Perhaps the kindest thing you can do is simply see them as individuals instead of "problems." Talk to them; see what they need. Even if you can't help them, your kind words and interest will do some good. Many homeless people are ignored and even a smile can make their day.

Action 15

Giving to the Homeless

If you are like many people we spoke to, you might not give money to people asking for a dollar to buy some food because you are skeptical about how the money will actually be spent. Most homeless people genuinely need assistance buying food and other necessities; there are a variety of ways that you can help.

What You Can Do

1. Carry gift certificates for local restaurants, delis, and fast-food establishments. By doing so you can avoid ignoring someone who needs your help and be sure that your money is going toward food.

2. Ask your friends and family to donate money to a local homeless shelter instead of giving you presents to celebrate your wedding, birthday, or other occasion.

3. Purchase *Street News,* a biweekly newspaper that helps the homeless help themselves. The publisher sells papers to individuals for twenty-five cents, which they in turn sell for a dollar apiece. For every paper sold, they earn an extra five cents that is

deposited in a special savings account set up by the publishers and earmarked for rent.

4. When you are making your lunch for the day, make an extra sandwich or add a piece of fruit to offer to a homeless person instead of money.

5. If you live in a state with a container law, you have probably seen people collecting beverage bottles and cans from garbage cans, off the streets, and sometimes from yards and businesses. The bottles may not mean a lot to you, but they could be the difference between eating and not eating to a homeless family. Collect your bottles and put them in a visible spot or drop them off at a local shelter.

6. Give old toys to a local shelter. Most homeless children do not have many possessions and their parents can't afford to buy them toys. Don't worry about the size of the toy—even a small yo-yo will be greatly appreciated.

7. Volunteer at a shelter or a soup kitchen. These organizations are almost always in need of volunteers. You can do anything from serving food to playing with youngsters. The homeless situation is so overwhelming that it is easy to feel that you as an individual couldn't possibly make a difference, but that isn't true. If you help only one person, you have accomplished a great thing.

The Children's Hope Foundation acts as a national clearinghouse for volunteers and maintains a data base of over 8,400 programs that would welcome your assistance. To find out how you can help, contact:

The Hope Foundation for the Homeless
P.O. Box 560908
Dallas, TX 75356-0908
(800) 843-4073

Other organizations you can contact for information about helping the homeless include:

National Alliance to End Homelessness
1518 K St., NW

Suite 206
Washington, DC 20005
(202) 638-1526

National Coalition for the Homeless
1612 K St., NW
Suite 1004
Washington, DC 20006
(202) 775-1322

Action 16
Habitat for Humanity

Habitat for Humanity is a Christian housing ministry that builds houses for families in danger of becoming homeless. The community chapter, acting as a bank, holds a no-interest loan on the house being built. The average cost to a family is $30,000 plus about five hundred hours of "sweat equity" (physical labor). The money is paid back in reasonable monthly installments of about $150, which are affordable for most working individuals. By requiring people to participate in the construction of their own homes, Habitat not only provides living quarters for people but teaches them valuable skills that will help them maintain the houses, and brings together people from the community who might never have met.

What You Can Do

Anyone can volunteer on a Habitat project. To find out about projects in your area, call your local chapter or contact the national chapter at:

Habitat for Humanity
121 Habitat St.
Americus, GA 31709-3498
(912) 924-6935

Part II

Raising the Next Generation

How to ensure that the next generation does a better job than we've done when they take over the reins, by making sure our schools are places where children really learn, by sharing with kids the best our world has to offer, and by helping them cope with the worst

Chapter 5

It Takes a Village to Raise a Child

To know the pleasure of slicing and dicing with a razor-sharp knife or trimming the rose bushes with freshly sharpened shears is to understand that well-cared-for tools make any job a lot easier. We don't mean to imply that today's children should be compared to a set of kitchen knives, but the truth is that their skills, perspectives, sensitivities, and desire to work for change are the tools that will shape the future for all of us. The sharper they are, the better.

An African proverb says, "It takes a village to raise a child." Whether we have children or not, the truth is that we're all responsible for looking out for the next generation and making sure that they get the love, support, understanding, and guidance they need to take over the reins when it's their turn to run things. Unfortunately, in our increasingly fast-paced society, many children are *not* getting the attention they need. At home, the average child spends more time in front of a television set than she or he does with a parent. In many schools formal education and extra-curricular activities have taken a backseat to

Sources for this section include: Jennifer Vogel, "Throw Away the Key," *Utne Reader,* July/Aug. 1994 (Minneapolis, MN); Amy Hatkoff and Karen Kelly Klopp, *How to Save the Children* (New York: Simon & Schuster, 1992).

discipline and safety measures. The results are nothing to cheer about: an estimated 2,700 babies are born into poverty every day; American students have the lowest test scores of any industrialized nation; teen suicides have increased 20 percent in the past decade; 250 kids a day are arrested for violent crimes; and a shrinking number of adequately trained, or trainable, young people enter the workforce every year.

But things certainly don't need to continue in this vein. There is little that's more resilient than the human spirit and a child's innate curiosity about the world. Take the example of an enlightened pilot program in an inner-city Baltimore school that not only succeeds in teaching every elementary school student to read, write, and do math, but has unexpectedly inspired many parents, themselves high school dropouts, to "drop in" and earn high school equivalencies. Another program, sponsored by Coca-Cola, successfully helps younger students learn basic skills, while dramatically decreasing the dropout rate among the high school students who tutor them. The list of success stories is impressive, inspiring, and growing by the day.

These programs were orchestrated by an education board and a large corporation, but they started with individuals who cared enough to make changes. There's plenty that you can do right now to help. Whether you are a parent yourself or just concerned, this section will tell you how you can get more involved in your school system, how to connect kids with nature and their own creativity, and how to help the kids who need it most.

Chapter 6

Saving Our Schools

According to the Children's Defense Fund, every eight seconds of every school day another student drops out. Talented men and women are leaving the teaching profession or shying away from the field altogether. Parents and businesspeople are up in arms about our public education system. What is to be done? Do we throw up our hands and say the situation is hopeless? No! The truth is that the involvement of parents, businesspeople, and other members of the community is already having a positive effect on the health of schools across the country. You, too, can be part of the solution.

Action 17

Volunteer Some Time at School

What's the single factor most likely to improve a child's grades? The surprising answer cuts across all racial and economic lines:

Sources for this section include: Thomas French, "Parents Are the Real Dropouts," *New York Times,* Aug. 23, 1993; Amy Hatkoff and Karen Kelly Klopp, *How to Save the Children* (New York: Simon & Schuster, 1992); Richard Louv, *101 Things You Can Do for Our Children's Future* (New York: Doubleday, 1994).

If a child's parent makes at least one visit to the school or attends one school function during the year, that child's grades are likely to improve. A parent involvement program, pioneered by the Yale Child Study Center, also showed a dramatic effect on dropout rates. The first school to implement the program saw the rate of students leaving school plummet from 42 percent to 15.5 percent and the number of kids going on for post-secondary schooling rise from 45 percent to 78 percent. Suspensions virtually disappeared.

A survey by the National Education Association found that more than 90 percent of teachers want parents to be more involved in education. In fact, parent indifference often rates above salary issues as the leading cause of dissatisfaction among our nation's teachers. According to the annual Metropolitan Life Survey of American Teachers, the majority of teachers believes that the number one priority in education policy should be to strengthen the role parents play in their children's education. The same survey found that 40 percent of teachers who were considering leaving education after completing two years in the classroom cited uncooperative parents as a significant reason.

Many educators have also found that the presence of parents has a far greater impact on maintaining discipline than security measures such as installing bars on windows and metal detectors at school entrances.

What You Can Do

Whether you're a parent or a concerned community member, there are plenty of ways to use your time and talents to help improve your local school.

Volunteer as a classroom aide: Your presence will allow teachers to work with students who need more attention. You'll also bring another perspective into the classroom; people learn in different ways, and your style may be the key to a struggling student's success.

Give a presentation on a hobby, trip, or job: No matter how outstanding a teacher is, she or he would welcome an outside boost to the curriculum. Arrange to show slides of a faraway place, give a concert on your favorite instrument, or make time to talk about your job on career day.

Become a tutor: One-on-one tutoring can make all the difference between success and failure for a child. Volunteers are badly needed in almost every school. Even if you don't think of yourself as a "teacher," your work as a tutor will be invaluable.

Attend school functions: Make time to see a school play, support the sports teams, or volunteer to chaperon kids on a trip to the museum. Kids want to feel that their activities are important not just to peers and teachers but to parents and neighbors as well.

Join the PTA: This will enable you to keep abreast with the goings-on at school and give you voting power. This is especially important when a school is searching for a new principal or vice principal. It has been shown time and time again that a single individual is generally behind the success of an innovative idea; helping choose the right principal can make all the difference to a child's education.

Call schools in your area or contact these resources for more information on getting involved:

Cities in Schools
1199 N. Fairfax St.
Suite 300
Alexandria, VA 22314-1963
(703) 519-8999
Find out how you can volunteer to provide a wide range of services in your local schools.

Help One Student to Succeed (HOSTS)
8000 NE Parkway Dr.

Suite 201
Vancouver, WA 98662
(800) 833-4678
Find out how you can help students master such fundamentals as reading, writing, and study skills.

Action 18

Your Life Experience Can Make Education Relevant

It is often difficult for kids to see the connection between what they learn in school and what matters in the world outside. As a member of the community, you can use your own experience to help students apply their skills to real-life situations. This is exactly what happened when Bill Stapp, of the University of Michigan's School of Natural Resources and Environment, visited a middle school in Detroit.

During an environmental education workshop he attended, kids were asked to discuss the most pressing issues in their local environment and some possible solutions to these problems. Then they were asked to choose one problem and to try to correct it. They decided to tackle a dangerous situation just beyond the school grounds: a busy highway that claimed the life of at least one student every year because the stoplight gave pedestrians only seven seconds to cross.

With Stapp to guide them, students petitioned the city to increase the amount of time they had to cross the street. They studied the structure of the local government and targeted the various departments they needed to go through to change a traffic light. Stapp and other adults who got involved were there only for support and to serve as references. The students did the entire project on their own, and in the end the light was changed. This exercise not only improved the school's safety and taught kids firsthand how government works, but also empowered the entire student body.

What You Can Do

When you or your business get requests from schools to provide speakers at events like the environmental education workshop Stapp attended, volunteer to go. You may not have time to work on a lengthy project, but even a few hours will help students see the importance of their education.

Another great approach is to make internships and apprenticeships available at your business. Spending a few hours a week, or even a month, to give students a taste of the business world can be a tremendous boon to their education. The following resources can help you and your business set up valuable partnerships with schools and individual students in your area.

Committee for Economic Development
477 Madison Ave.
New York, NY 10022
(212) 688-2063
The committee can help your business establish partnerships with area schools that can help solve problems in your community.

National Association of Partners in Education, Inc.
209 Madison St.
Suite 401
Alexandria, VA 22314
(703) 836-4880
The association assists businesses, schools, and communities in establishing partnerships. Call for more information.

Action 19

Get Involved with School Maintenance

Appearance is very important to kids. This extends to every aspect of their lives, including their school building. Many school facilities in this country are in poor shape, partly as the result of vandalism. Kids are going to leave their mark, but when they believe that the environment belongs to them, the mark is far more likely to be a positive one. One school in south-central Los Angeles proved the point by involving students, parents, and neighbors in the transformation of school grounds into a series of gardens. When the Los Angeles riots hit, school buildings were destroyed, but no one touched the gardens.

Students may be skeptical at first, but seeing parents and neighbors working hard to clean up and repair their school may motivate them to pitch in and give them a greater sense of taking responsibility for what is theirs. Community labor not only improves morale, but frees school funds for other activities and accomplishes projects that might not otherwise happen. At one La Jolla, California, elementary school, parents circumvented an unresponsive school system bureaucracy to make life more pleasant for their children. Many students suffered bad sunburns when they sat outside to eat their lunch. Unable to get the school district to devise a source of shade, the principal enlisted the help of parents. They raised $2,000 and built a shade system themselves. Had the school system hired contractors to do the same job, the $40,000 cost would have had to come out of the elementary school's budget.

Action 20

Halt the Commercialization of Our Schools

The science class lesson for the day is geothermic "gushers": volcanoes, geysers and hot springs. The teacher passes out a free education program, "Gushers, Wonder of the World," produced and distributed by Lifetime Learning Systems on behalf of Gusher Fruit Snacks Co. The "Extended Activities" section suggests that students bite into a free sample of Gusher fruit snacks. "How does this process differ from that which produces erupting geothermic phenomena?" Lifetime Learning proposes that teachers ask their students.

Gusher's marketing program is only one of countless free "educational" packets sent to teachers by marketing firms, like Lifetime Learning Systems, hired to promote a corporation's product or image. Since 1979 the corporate educational movement has flourished and more and more educators are jumping on the marketing bandwagon. Consumers Union reported in 1990 that twenty million school students a year use corporate-sponsored teaching materials.*

Although some corporations have created stellar programs to help kids stay in school and go on to higher education, many view classrooms as captive audiences of potential consumers. Indeed, with children and teenagers buying $90 billion worth of consumer goods every year, and influencing the buying decisions made by their parents, it's no surprise that corporations are vying for the chance to influence our young consumers.

What You Can Do

Here are some actions to take to save your local school from being overrun by advertisements.

1. Attend school board meetings and ask for a list of all sponsored materials.
2. Ask your school board to develop guidelines governing the use of sponsored materials which, at the minimum, require that they be subject to the same evaluation procedures as other parts of the school curriculum.
3. Tell advertisers that you will not purchase products marketed in schools.
4. Write to your representatives and demand that school-based advertising be made taxable.

*Excerpted with permission from Dr. Alex Molnar, "Corporations in the Classroom," *Co-op America Quarterly*, Winter 1994. Co-op America is a non-profit membership organization dedicated to building a sustainable economy based on peace, justice, cooperation, and the health of the environment. For more information, write 1850 M St., NW, Suite 700, Washington, DC 20036, or telephone (202) 872-5307.

For more information, consult the following:

Consumers Union
Education Services
101 Truman Ave.
Yonkers, NY 10703-1057
To order a copy of its pamphlet Selling America's Kids, *send $2.*

Read *Civics for Democracy,* by Ralph Nader, which advocates the reform of civic education. Available from Essential Books, P.O. Box 19405, Washington, DC 20036.

Chapter 7

At Home

If you have kids, you've probably experienced the anguish and disappointment of not spending as much time with them as you'd like for a slew of reasons: long hours at work; TV, video games, and other high-tech stimuli vying for their attention; playdates; your own need to spend time alone or with your partner or friends. If you aren't a parent, you've probably sympathized with friends and relatives who are trying to balance full schedules and still make time for the children.

During the past twenty-five years, as the world has gotten more complex, the average amount of time parents spend with their children has dropped by 40 percent. According to the Family Research Council, the average parent now spends just seventeen hours a week with his or her children, and this includes meal time and chauffeuring, as well as whatever time is left for reading, playing, and talking. Here are some ways to do the most for the kids in this limited amount of time, whether they be sons and daughters, nieces and nephews, or your friends' offspring.

Sources for this section include: Susan Allen Toth, "The Overscheduled Child," *Family Life*, March/April 1994 (New York, NY); Richard Louv, *101 Things You Can Do for Our Children's Future* (New York: Doubleday, 1994).

Action 21

Don't Overprogram the Kids

To keep the creative juices flowing, we all need occasional free time to do absolutely nothing. This is particularly true for children. When kids don't get the opportunity for unstructured play and exploration, they don't learn to explore their own thoughts and dreams. Not only will they lack self-understanding, but they will not develop the necessary skills for self-entertainment and as a result will never be really comfortable alone.

Some parents, in an effort to give their children every advantage, fill up all free time with organized activities. While activities are wonderful for teaching kids skills and how to work with others, too much of a good thing will work against a child in the long run. Why we do this comes, in part, from a Puritan heritage that frowns on idleness and in part from the dangers our modern world presents.

Whereas children of past generations could safely wander into some nearby woods or fields to while away the hours alone or with friends, fewer children today have access to wild places, and fewer parents would approve of these solo excursions, even where the opportunity exists. But even if the neighborhood woods are gone, a climbing tree in the backyard or a private bedroom can make a fine refuge.

What You Can Do

Make sure kids have unscheduled time when the TV and video games are off-limits. At first they may have a very difficult time with this and complain that they're bored. Resist the temptation to give them projects or make suggestions. Let them figure it out for themselves. Keep at it. Eventually they'll begin to tap into the internal world that holds the key to imagination and creative play. After a while you may start wondering if they're spending *too much* time "doing nothing." They aren't; they're engaged in the serious business of getting to know themselves, so let them enjoy it!

Action 22

Introducing Children to Nature

Many kids today can wax far more eloquently than their parents about the threats to our planet. But fewer and fewer children are developing a deep connection to their own local environments. This is a disturbing trend, because the level of concern adults have for the environment is heavily influenced by their exposure to the natural world when they were children.

People are not born with a love of nature; a child has to experience nature firsthand before he or she can learn to appreciate it. One Baltimore schoolteacher discovered this for himself when he invited members of his inner-city class to join him for a nature walk in rural Maryland. Much to his surprise, these junior high students, for whom drugs, handguns, and AIDS were part of daily life, were terrified of the woods. Even birdcalls made them uncomfortable. But many of the kids were brave enough to join subsequent outings and soon found themselves totally at home in what had once been a threatening environment. These kids will most likely grow up with a love and respect for nature that their friends may never develop.

What You Can Do

1. Make sure the kids in your life get a chance to bond with nature. If you live in a city, make a point of spending time in green spaces or get out of town when possible to a place with lots of nooks and crannies to explore.

    You can help kids get connected by making a game out of learning to identify plants, bird songs, or insects. If you stumble across something that no one knows about, encourage one of the kids to do some research and report back. This will further encourage a lifelong interest in nature.

    If you visit land where you have permission to dig up ferns, moss, and other plant life, introduce the kids to terrarium building, which is a also good way to teach them about ecosystems.

Camps, scout troops, outing clubs, and environmental education programs are also excellent ways to give children access to nature. Contact any of the following resources to find out what's happening in your area:

The American Hiking Society
P.O. Box 20160
Washington, DC 20041-2160
(703) 255-9304

Boy Scouts of America
345 Hudson St.
New York, NY 10014
(212) 242-1100

Camp Fire Boys and Girls
4601 Madison Ave.
Kansas City, MO 64112
(816) 756-1950

4-H Program and Youth Development
Extension Service
U.S. Department of Agriculture
7100 Connecticut Ave.
Chevy Chase, MD 20815
(301) 961-2800

Girl Scouts of the USA
43 W. 23rd St.
New York, NY 10010
(212) 645-4000

North American Association for Environmental Education
Dept. A.
P.O. Box 400
Troy, OH 45373

2. Get kids involved in their own environmental groups. It's a great way to make them feel like they're part of the solution and to help them develop a level of care and understanding for the earth that will last a lifetime.

The Cousteau Society, Inc.
870 Greenbrier Circle
Suite 402
Chesapeake, VA 23320
(804) 523-9335
The society publishes the bimonthly magazine Dolphin Log *for its younger members (free with a family membership or $10 for a subscription).*

Kids against Pollution
P.O. Box 775, High St.
Closter, NJ 07624
(201) 784-0668
KAP features a newsletter that gives kids a forum for exchanging success stories about their antipollution efforts.

National Geographic Society
17th and M Sts., NW
Washington, DC 20036
(202) 857-7000
National Geographic publishes a magazine just for kids called World *($12.95 a year for twelve issues).*

National Wildlife Federation
1400 16th St., NW
Washington, DC 20036-2266
(202) 797-6800
NWF publishes two monthly magazines for children: Ranger Rick *for kids 6 to 12 ($14/yr. for twelve issues) and* Big Backyard *($10/yr. for twelve issues) for 3-year-olds.*

3. Kids with access to computers and modems will want to investigate:

EnviroNet
Greenpeace Action
139 Townsend, 4th Floor
San Francisco, CA 94107
Dial with a modem (415) 512-9108 to get on-line
(415) 512-9025
A computer network just for kids that features conferences on topics concerning the environment.

Chapter 8

Toys, TV, Games, and Entertainment

Action 23
Alternatives to High-Tech Entertainment

Recent studies show that playing video games may actually make reading more difficult, because it trains the eyes in a completely different set of skills. Studies have also shown that even a few hours of watching violence on TV makes kids more prone to fighting. Moderate amounts of time spent watching television and playing video games are probably necessary for a child to stay current with his or her peers (see Actions 24 and 26). But there are plenty of low-tech ways to keep the kids entertained that will bring the family together and stimulate parts of the brain that high-tech entertainment does not.

What You Can Do

1. Make sure everyone has a library card. Family outings to the library can be fun and are a good way for family members to

Sources for this section include: Dorian Friedman, "Good Guys and Bad Guys Fight for Control: The Politics of Children's TV" and Bob Strauss, "Family Matters: "Getting a Grip on Video Game Madness," *Family Life*, Dec./Jan. 1994; Bruce DeSilva, "TV More Violent than Ever," *Hartford Courant*, Oct. 12, 1987 (Hartford, CT); Susan Finnie Rockwell, "Computers: Serious Fun," *Atlantic Monthly*, April 1994 (Boston, MA).

learn more about one another's interests. A child is far more likely to grow up to be an avid reader if reading is a natural part of family life.

2. Let the kids subscribe to their own magazines. Kids love to get mail and many may prefer to read articles rather than books. Magazines like *Ranger Rick* have plenty of short, well-illustrated articles written specifically for young readers. Borrow a variety of children's publications from your public library, and then let your kids choose for themselves.

3. Tell stories. Storytelling used to be the way information was passed from one generation to the next. Children would be entertained with vivid recollections of family history, tall tales, and fantasy. Telling stories is more than just good fun: it helps children develop their imagination. Unlike TV, where everything is spelled out, listening to stories allows children to decide for themselves what characters and places look like. Encouraging children to tell their own stories builds confidence and inspires creativity.

4. Develop the art of conversation. Give children ample opportunity to talk about the things they are learning in school and in their outside reading. Share information about your life—talk about what you're learning at work, what books you're reading, and how your friends are doing. Just as children need lots of practice to learn to speak, they also need help learning to converse.

5. Play games. Games of all kinds help children develop good sportsmanship and have fun. If you're not much of a games person, consult some books for ideas. You and the kids can decide together what new games to learn or ask your child to pick out a game, learn the rules, and teach you. Play groups are great for parents with young kids.

There are wonderful activity books on the market and in your library that can help you and your kids find creative ways to have fun. Here's just a sampling of what's available:

Kids & Weekends: Creative Ways to Make Special Days, by Avery Hart and Paul Mantell (Charlotte, VT: Williamson Publishing, 1992)

The Kids' Nature Book, 365 Indoor/Outdoor Activities and Experiences,
by Susan Milord (Charlotte, VT: Williamson Publishing,
1989)

365 Outdoor Activities You Can Do with Your Child, by Steve and
Ruth Bennett (Holbrook, MA: Bob Adams, Inc., 1993)

365 TV-Free Activities You Can Do with Your Child, by Steve and
Ruth Bennett (Holbrook, MA: Bob Adams, Inc., 1991)

Action 24

Reducing Violence on Television

Children's television has included violent offerings for decades.
Classic cartoons like *Tom and Jerry* and *Woody Woodpecker*, introduced over thirty years ago, average twenty violent acts per
show. But that's nothing compared to today's programs for children. According to the Center for Media and Public Affairs,
while prime-time network programs for adults average two to
three violent acts per hour, children's cartoons and toy commercials are an average of five times more violent, with some
cartoons reaching as many as eighty-four separate acts of violence per show!

There's no question that kids are watching violence on TV—
as many as twelve thousand violent acts a year—but is it really
hurting them? Probably. Studies seem to show that watching
violence does produce antisocial behavior in children. In one
typical study, a group of four-year-olds were shown *Batman* and
Superman cartoons every day for four weeks, while a second
group of children watched *Mr. Rogers' Neighborhood,* and a third
group watched educational films. The children who viewed violent cartoons exhibited greater tendencies to hit other children,
call people names, and refuse to obey classroom rules.

Children's television enjoyed a golden era in the 1970s when
after-school educational specials and short educational piece
like ABC's *Schoolhouse Rock!* were regular fare. But times
have changed. Reagan-era deregulation of the Federal
Communications Commission led to the near disappearance of
educational programming and the rise of shows that are little

more than toy commercials. In 1980, networks aired at least eleven hours a week of educational programs for children. By 1992 you'd be hard pressed to find an hour a week of educational fare for children, whereas the best-selling children's toys all had their own TV shows.

Doesn't anyone see that deregulation has been a disaster; shouldn't the government do something about it? The fact is that five years of crusading by Peggy Charren, founder of Action for Children's Television, and other advocates led to the 1990 passage of the Children's Television Act, designed to limit the number of commercials that can be aired during children's programming and to increase educational and informational offerings. Unfortunately, the law has had minimal effect. Commercial time has dropped from as much as 14 minutes per hour down to 10.5 minutes per hour on weekends and 12 minutes per hour during the week, but efforts to expand educational programming have been feeble. In their applications to the FCC for license renewals, broadcasters have included *Leave It to Beaver* and *The Jetsons* on the list of educational shows. Some wonderful programming has been produced since the law went into effect—but much of it has aired between 5:30 and 7:00 A.M.! Needless to say, these efforts have not satisfied children's advocates.

What You Can Do

1. Write to Congress: Ask your state's representatives and senators to support strict enforcement of the Children's Television Act. Write to your members of Congress at the U.S. House of Representatives, Washington, DC 20515, and to the U.S. Senate, Washington, DC 20510. (To find out who your representative is, you can call the House Cloakroom at [202] 225-3121.)

2. Watch what your children watch. Teach them to be critical of what they see and to think about what they are being told. If you or your children are not happy with what you see on your local station, contact: Federal

Communications Commission, Mass Media Bureau, Complaints and Investigations, 1919 M St., NW, Washington, DC 20554; (202) 632-7048.

3. For $5, you can order *When Pulling the Plug Isn't Enough: A Parent's Guide to TV* from the Center for Media Education, 1511 K St., NW, Suite 518, Washington, DC 20005; (202) 628-2620.

Action 25

"Bang! Bang! You're Dead": Toys of War and Destruction

Toy machine guns, death ray guns, tanks, war-making robots and spaceships, stimulate hostile, brutal feelings even in very young children, which gradually erode their capacities for tenderness and sympathy.—Dr. Benjamin Spock

Every time we purchase a toy, we communicate our adult values to the children who receive these toys. Through play, children imitate our values. Do we want children to assume that war has a positive value to us by letting them play with war toys? Do we want them to think that disputes and differences are best settled by force, and that the world is divided up into good guys and bad guys?

We may not be able to shelter children from all forms of violent play. They may still hold out a finger to imitate a gun. But we need to explain to children, at their own level of understanding, the meaning and consequences of real war—that real people don't get up when shot with a real gun.

Mechanized war toys do not require or develop courage or creative problem solving. They are substitutes for courage. They lead children to think that everything can be settled by pushing a button or pulling a trigger. Today, when war has become destroyer of whole populations, we must stop encouraging children to make a game of killing, especially with toys of destruction.

55

Parents need to realize that the major objection to war toys is that they condition children to accept something that is unacceptable. If, as adults, they try to use these weapons to settle differences, they will fail, and the human race will be the victim.*

What You Can Do

1. Write a letter to the editor of your local paper urging people not to buy war toys for their children.
2. Speak with family, friends, and especially other parents, encouraging them not to buy war toys.
3. Meet with the manager of your local toy store, share your thoughts, and urge the store to stop carrying war toys.
4. The New England War Registers League has initiated a campaign against war toys and cartoons. The organization has published a brochure called *Killers in Your Toy Box* that describes this campaign and gives specific examples of ways that you can get involved. To receive this brochure and other information, contact the organization at:

New England War Resisters League
339 Lafayette St.
New York, NY 10012
(212) 228-0450

5. Also available from the War Resisters League is a complete list of war toy manufacturers as well as a list of alternative toy, book, and music manufacturers whose products are available by direct mail.
6. Companies listen to people who buy their products—they are, after all, dependent on their support. Why not write them a note or give them a call? It is a good idea to give

*Excerpted with permission from "You and Your Children," by Carol Jahnkow, Stop War Toys Campaign, New England War Resisters League.

positive as well as negative comments about their products. Below are the addresses and phone numbers of the three largest toy companies in the United States.

Hasbro, Inc.
1027 Newport Ave.
Pawtucket, RI 02862
Stephen Hassenfed, President
(609) 234-7400

Mattel, Inc.
333 Continental Blvd.
El Segundo, CA 90245
Jill Barad, President
(800) 524-8697

Tyco Toys, Inc.
6000 Midlantic Drive, 2d Floor
Mount Laurel, NJ 08054
Richard Grey, CEO
(800) 367-8926

Action 26

Computer Games and Video Violence

Ever since the introduction of Space Invaders many years ago, toy and game manufacturers have exploited the profit potential of computers and video games which all too often bring additional violence into the lives of children. The latest wave of games out in the marketplace is far more sophisticated and realistic.

These descendants of Space Invaders are available for most every type of home computer and video game system. Children and adults can spend time blowing away anything from steroid-pumped animals and fellow human beings in order to save humanity, the earth, or themselves from certain death and destruction.

Of great importance to war toy opponents—are "simulations," games that attempt in varying degrees to create the impression of a "true experience" that can be related to the player's knowledge of the real world.*

These range from games in which the player must bomb an out-of-favor foreign nation and destroy its people to games that depict brutal street fights. Playing these games may be more detrimental to your child than watching violence on television, a pastime that often leads to increased violence in children. This is due in part to the fact that unlike television, these games are not passive but require active participation.

Two especially violent video games became available in the fall of 1993: Sega's "Night Trap" and Acclaim Entertainment's "Mortal Kombat." "Night Trap," which acts out bloody attacks on young women, was eventually taken off the shelves of Toys "R" Us, F.A.O. Schwarz, and some other retailers in the middle of the Christmas season. Although Sega removed "Night Trap" from the market in January 1994, it is planning to release an edited version.

Luckily the same sophistication that has made these games possible has also led to the release of a variety of creative, non-violent alternative games. Unlike the situation a few years ago, it is now possible to play video games that don't require you to become a juvenile Genghis Khan. So exercise caution when you shop for video games. Video cartridges can now be rented from most local video stores, so pay attention to what your child brings home.

What You Can Do

1. Write letters of protest to:

Toy Manufacturers of America
200 Fifth Ave.

*Excerpted with permission from Larry Erickson, "Video Violence," for the New England War Resisters League.

Suite 740
New York, NY 10010
(212) 675-1141

Let this group know that you want its members to eliminate their violent toys and games.

2. Contact the New England War Resisters League, 339 Lafayette St., New York, NY 10012; (212) 228-0450, to learn more about its war toys information package and "Children, Youth, and Nonviolence" package, both of which include addresses of companies you can write to protest.

3. Protest to your local toy store. Many videos now have a rating system not unlike that of movies. Although the effectiveness of this rating system is questionable, it does provide you with some guidelines. But most video and toy stores will rent or sell these videos to children regardless of the ratings. Make sure that toy stores are aware of the system and that they enforce it.

4. Get your kids hooked on video games that are fun and also good for them. There are an increasing number of video games on the market that are engrossing and entertaining without being violent or demeaning. "SimCity," for example, teaches kids to manage an urban metropolis, giving points based on, among other things, pollution index, popularity with taxpayers, and the crime rate. These games offer open-ended exploration and require a level of mastery that will keep kids just as entertained as their violent counterparts.

A sampling of some of the best available video games and computer programs for kids:

"Kid Pix" (Broderbund): ages 4 and up
"Millie's Math House" (Edmark): ages 2–6
"Oregon Trail" (MECC): ages 10–adult
"Reader Rabbit Series" (Learning Company): ages 5–8
"SimLife" (Maxis): ages 10–adult
"SimCity" (Maxis): ages 10–adult

Chapter 9

In Your Community and Beyond

K ids need room to find their own way in the world, but they also need adults to help support and guide them. Many kids who don't get that support at home could use your help.

Action 27
Getting to Know the Kids in Your Neighborhood

A childless couple moved into a neighborhood with lots of children and very little adult supervision. Faced with the prospect of threatening the kids who constantly ran through their yard and thus cutting themselves off from the neighborhood, they took a different tack. Within a few weeks they were on a first-name basis with most of the kids. They quickly established rules about when children could visit them and eventually allowed a number of the kids to plants small garden plots in the front yard, something the kids would not have been encouraged to do at home.

Sources for this section include: Amy Hatkoff and Karen Kelly Klopp, *How to Save the Children* (New York: Simon & Schuster, 1992).

With the growing number of latchkey kids who return from school to empty houses, all neighborhoods have kids who could use befriending. While many kids have access to after-school programs, others do not. Being at home alone can be scary for children, especially if they don't know they have a safe place to turn for help if they need it.

What You Can Do

Volunteer to help out at after-school programs in local schools, youth organizations, or the YMCA/YWCA. Get to know the kids on your block, make sure they know your name and phone number (if you're comfortable with this), and let them know that they should come to you in case of an emergency.

In the Chicago area a program called "Grandma Please" links latchkey children with older volunteers who are delighted to have phone pals to talk to in the afternoons. It's a great support system for both the kids and the adults, many of whom are homebound. For information on setting up a similar program in your area, contact:

Marcia Glaser
Director of Senior Programs
Wholehouse Association
4520 N. Beacon St.
Chicago, IL 60640
(312) 561-3500

Action 28

Helping the Kids Who Need It the Most

The sad truth is that while many children in America are happily going about the business of growing up, many others face abuse and neglect. Over 100,000 of our children are homeless and every 32 seconds another baby is born into poverty. Every 13 seconds a child is reported abused or neglected; every 13 hours a preschooler is murdered. Kids are dropping out of

61

school at an unprecedented rate; one in four never finishes high school. One in eight seventeen-year-olds has reading and writing skills that are below the sixth-grade level, so that these children are classified as functionally illiterate.

For kids who are "at risk," growing up in poverty, and surrounded by violence, there are few, if any, opportunities to change their lives for the better. As adults they will almost certainly face more poverty, crime, and violence. Reaching out to just one of these kids, or lending your support to one of the many fine organizations dedicated to helping them, can make an immeasurable difference. Robert, an eighteen-year-old prisoner at the Rikers Island penitentiary, speaks to all of us when he says, "If just one person had paid me some attention, my life would have been totally different."

What You Can Do

1. Most of us can afford to take the basic necessities of life for granted, but for many children food, shelter, and clothing are often unavailable. The following organizations can help you fill these basic needs for a child:

   The Campaign to End Childhood Hunger
   Food Research & Action Center
   1875 Connecticut Ave., NW
   Suite #540
   Washington, DC 20009
   (202) 986-2200
   Contact them to find about hunger programs in your area.

   The Box Project
   P.O. Box 435
   Dept. BP
   Plainville, CT 06062
   Write to find out how you can help supply families with much-needed clothing and other household items.

Habitat for Humanity
121 Habitat St.
Americus, GA 31709-3498
(912) 924-6935
Call to find out how you can join its efforts to build and renovate housing for people in need.

NGA
1007 B St. Rd.
Southhampton, PA 18966
(215) 322-5759
NGA gets clothing and other essential items to those in need. Call to see if it has a program in your area.

To find out how to start your own program to get clothing to kids, contact:

Connie Kennedy
(914) 576-6053
In 1991 her Back-to-School Clothes project saw to it that 640 children had new clothes for school.

Clothing banks have been established in a number of states to distribute new clothing, donated by manufactures, to homeless and needy families. Call (404) 521-0530 for more information on setting up a program in your area.

2. Kids at risk rarely have positive role models or anyone who can really spend time and energy on them alone. If you can spare even a few hours a month to be a mentor for a child, you will have a dramatic effect on his or her life. Any of the following organizations can help you.

Big Brothers/Big Sisters of America
230 N. 13th St.
Philadelphia, PA 19107
(215) 567-7000

Foster Grandparent Program
Corporation for National Service
1100 Vermont Ave., NW, 6th Floor
Washington, D.C. 20525
Telephone: (202) 606-4849
Fax: (202) 606-4854

The National Media Outreach Center
The Plus Project on Mentoring
4802 Fifth Ave.
Pittsburgh, PA 15213
(412) 622-1491

3. Tutoring is a great way to spend time with a child and also to give him or her skills that will make it possible to stay in school. The following organization can put you in touch with children who could use your help.

Help One Student to Succeed (HOSTS)
1801 D St.
Vancouver, WA 98663-3332
(800) 833-4678

4. Become involved in a dropout prevention program in your area, and help kids finish their education.

The National Dropout Prevention Center
205 Martin St.
Clemson University
Clemson, SC 29634-5111
(803) 656-2599

Action 29

Be a Voice for Children in Congress

Children don't have a voice in Congress, yet every year important pieces of legislation come up that directly affect their lives.

In Your Community and Beyond

Immunization programs, child care, Head Start, child support enforcement, the nutritional content of school lunches—these and many other issues are affected by legislation.

Children need advocates who are willing to follow national legislation that affects them and who will lobby on their behalf. Small actions, like phone calls and postcards to members of Congress, can produce impressive results on crucial votes.

What You Can Do

Ben & Jerry's, the ice cream people, and the Children's Defense Fund have created the Call for Kids Campaign to keep you informed about child-related legislation. Before important votes, the campaign will advise you on whom to contact to make your voice heard.

Call for Kids Campaign
c/o Ben & Jerry's
Box 240
Waterbury, VT 05676
(800) 255-4371

Children's Defense Fund
25 E St., NW
Washington, DC 20001
(202) 628-8787

Part III

Computer Activism

How you can support legislation, communicate with the White House, protect prisoners of conscience, and help save the environment—all from the comfort of your own home

Chapter 10

Bridging the Gap between Information and Action

Computers were born and raised by the armed forces and popularized by the consumer economy. But their greatest value may prove to be neither military nor commercial.

The machines were first applied to massive mathematical problems for which the military wanted answers, such as explaining the turbulence created by atomic explosions or predicting the flight of artillery shells. For a quarter-century, computers were regarded as exotic machines that could be understood and operated only by geniuses.

But computers have changed, and so have their roles. No longer the exclusive province of a technical priesthood, they are just beginning to fulfill their destined purpose as organizers in an age of information glut. Their value lies in their ability to sort an overwhelming mass of raw industri-

Sources for this section include: Lester Brown et al., *State of the World* (New York: Norton, 1994); Adam C. Engst, *Internet Starter Kit* (Indianapolis: Hayden Books, 1993); Frances Moore Lappé and Paul Martin DuBois, *Quickening of America* (San Francisco: Jossey-Bass, 1994); Kellyn S. Betts, "The Coming Green Computers," *E Magazine*, March/April 1994 (*E Magazine* is a publication of Earth Action Network, Norwalk, CT); EcoNet.

al, economic, demographic, and scientific data into forms that can be used to solve problems.

The capacity of the computer to help us bridge the critical gap between information and knowledge is illustrated by the recent history of climate science. Scientists have theorized since 1896 that emissions of carbon from the burning of fossil fuels could warm the global atmosphere. It was not until the early eighties, however, that they were able to test their theories. Performing in minutes calculations that would take an unaided scientist a lifetime, supercomputers are able to give us a handle on incredibly complex problems, such as the effects of increased greenhouse gas concentrations in our atmosphere.

Computers offer enormous power for organizing information that can help effect positive change. In 1986, for example, U.S. environmentalists fought for and saw created the world's most comprehensive pollution database produced by the U.S. government—the Toxics Release Inventory (TRI), which was then used by activists to stimulate industrial cleanup.*

Computers have also opened incredible doors to communication and activism. In 1980 there were fewer than 2 million computers in the world. Today there are almost 150 million computers in use, 11 million of which are equiped with modems that allow them to communicate with one another. This unprecedented access to information and global communication puts you in a uniquely wonderful position to take action.

In this section you'll learn how to practice computer activism, lower your environmental impact when you compute, find a home for an outdated computer, and pressure the computer industry into cleaning up its act.

*Reprinted with permission from Lester Brown et al., *State of the World: A Worldwide Institute Report on Progress toward a Sustainable Society* (New York: Norton, 1994).

Network Activism

The beauty of computer activism is how easily and rapidly you can get your message across and stay up-to-date on important issues. Without leaving your keyboard you can notify hundreds, even thousands, of concerned citizens about the need to send a message to their representatives in Congress before a crucial vote, you can find out what's on the agenda at the United Nations, or you can let the president know what's on your mind.

Action 30

Getting Started on the Information Highway

The global computer network known as the Internet was developed in 1969 to connect scientists at U.S. computer centers who were doing defense-related research. It was adopted by academic and corporate communities and from there burgeoned into the global matrix that today links millions of computers in over fifty nations. The fantastic resources available on the Internet include the catalogs of the Library of Congress, thousands of specialized databases, a growing number of journals, and electronic bulletin boards that link users all over the world, discussing every topic imaginable.

If you adopt the image of the Internet as an information "superhighway," services such as Prodigy, CompuServe, and America Online are the toll booths you need to go through to gain access. These commercial services, are smaller, more easily navigated information sources than the Internet itself; most also serve as gateways to the Internet and allow you to send electronic mail (E-mail).

All you need to start communicating with people all over the world is access to a computer with a modem and some type of gateway service (see Action 31 for more about services).

If you are in the market for a computer, see Action 33 to learn more about the new generation of "green" computers.

Before you purchase a modem, try to determine what your needs will be. Typically, the more expensive the modem, the faster you can send and receive information. For less than $100 you can get a basic model (2400 baud) that will allow you to read information posted on electronic bulletin boards, send E-mail, and copy information from the networks onto your computer. But if you plan to use your modem a lot, you'll save time and long-distance charges by investing in a faster modem (9600 baud and up).

What You Can Do

Before you buy anything, get your hands on a book to help you understand what the Internet is and how this fascinating communications system works. The more you understand from the start, the less likely you are to get frustrated, and the sooner you can jump into computer activism with both feet.

Some recommended books for beginners are:

The Internet Companion Plus: A Beginner's Start-Up Kit for Global Networking, by Tracy Laquey (Reading, MA: Addison-Wesley, 1993).

The Internet Complete Reference, by Harley Hahn and Rick Stout (Berkeley: Osborne McGraw-Hill, 1993).

The Internet Guide for New Users, by Daniel Dern (New York: McGraw-Hill, 1994).

Internet Starter Kit for Macintosh, by Adam Engst (Indianapolis: Hayden Press, 1993).

The Online User's Encyclopedia: Bulletin Boards and Beyond, by Bernard Aboba (Reading, MA: Addison-Wesley, 1994).

Action 31
Selecting an On-line Service

Services such as America Online, CompuServe, and Prodigy let you do all kinds of fun things. Each has its own set of "forums," which are places to look for information and people interested in a particular topic. For example, if you're a CompuServe subscriber who's interested in environmental issues, you'll find like-minded users through the Earth Forum. You can use forums to gain access to information, to post inquiries, and to reply to other people's questions. Some forums even operate "conferences," which are live conversations that any subscriber can contribute to. Most services also let you send electronic mail (E-mail) to anyone who is connected to the Internet.

When you subscribe to a service you are, in a sense, joining a club. If you're interested in a wide range of topics, you'll probably want to join one of the big commercial services. But if you want to connect with people who have a strong interest in environmental and social issues, you may be more interested in one of the services that are specially geared toward these topics.

What You Can Do

There are plenty of books that can give you an idea of what the large commercial services have to offer. Here's a brief description of some of the more specialized services you might want to consider.

Institute for Global Communications (IGC) By far the biggest player in activist networking, with users all over the world, this is the primary network used by groups like Amnesty International and Peace Action. Just about everyone who's involved with peace, justice, and environmental issues has some interaction with this network.

IGC offers its users not one network but a family of "nets" that seems to be growing. At this writing the family includes PeaceNet, EcoNet, ConflictNet, and LaborNet. Conferences, or subsets of these main networks, could fill pages and are springing up constantly, as the needs of users change. For example, people interested in community issues will want to check out CommuNet on ConflictNet. If you're interested in Environmental Justice, you'll find a conference just for you residing on the EcoNet. For more information about what's available and how to join, write or call IGC at:

Institute for Global Communications
18 de Boon
San Francisco, CA 94107
(415) 442-0220

The TogetherNet An up-and-coming network with a rapidly growing subscriber base, TogetherNet has themes similar to IGC's, but at the time of this writing it's easier to use because of its graphical interface (graphic images that guide you around the different screen—IGC also has plans for a graphical interface). One of the more intriguing features is TogetherNet's direct link to the United Nations; you can get a morning update of what's going on at the UN, send E-mail to the delegates before important votes, give input on matters of importance to you, and so on. For more information about TogetherNet, write or phone:

Together Foundation
130 S. Willard St.
Burlington, VT 05401
(802) 862-2030

HandsNet Primarily geared toward human service and public interest organizations, HandsNet promotes information exchange, collaboration, and advocacy among individuals working on issues of social and justice reform. Also an easy-to-use graphical interface system, this net deals with topics including hunger and nutrition, health care, poverty and economic development, and agriculture. Contact:

HandsNet
20195 Stevens Creek Blvd.
Suite 120

Cupertino, CA 95014
(408) 257-4500

For more information about environmentally oriented computer services, consult *Ecolinking: Everyone's Guide to Online Environmental Information,* by Don Rittner (Berkeley: Peachpit Press, 1992).

Action 32

Getting In on the Action without Saying a Word

Once you're on-line, there's no end to the good you can do. Generally, here are your options:

1. You can read and post information.
2. You can respond to calls for action and post your own.
3. You can send E-mail to anyone with an E-mail address.

All the News—before It Hits Print

For die hard news junkies, or anyone who enjoys substance, on-line information is a refreshing change from mass media programs. Because forums provide a place for people with shared interests to exchange information and engage in lively debate, the content has real value.

On any given day you can read reports on the Internet that may not show up in the *New York Times* for days. And much of what you'll read may never be available anywhere else. During the Gulf War, while the television brought dramatic shots of tense network celebrities describing the drama with Scud missiles exploding in the background, many Internet users experienced the war more intimately, through the words of ordinary Israeli citizens who were sitting at their computers recording history from their perspective.

Quiet Voices that Speak Volumes

Another beautiful thing about computer activism is that you don't need a forceful personality to be a strong voice for change. If you can string sentences together in a clear, readable fashion, you can make your views known. Unlike public hearings or town meetings, there's room for everyone, and you don't need public speaking skills.

Computers allow you to reach large numbers of people all at once, which can make activism less time-consuming. Dave Hughes, a laptop activist in Colorado, can testify to this. When fighting the revision of a local ordinance, he enlisted the help of fellow citizens via a computer network. He typed up information about the proposed ordinance change and put it on-line. He explained why he didn't like the change and asked readers to join him at the next planning commission meeting. One hundred and seventy-five people showed up! As a result, the ordinance was changed to one that the community supported.

Amnesty International also reports impressive responses to network calls to action. On January 12, 1994, Amnesty issued to supporters in New Zealand, Australia, Finland, Great Britain, Italy, Mexico, the Netherlands, and the Philippines an "Urgent Action" appeal on behalf of an Iranian citizen named Mehdi Dibaj, who was at imminent risk of execution. On January 18 Dibaj was released. While no one can say what role Amnesty supporters played in his release, it is likely that E-mail helped save his life.

The Environmental Lawyers Alliance Worldwide (E-LAW) used E-mail to enhance Peru's constitution. By connecting with members worldwide, Jorge Gutierrez of E-LAW Peru collected the information needed to ensure that the Peruvian constitution now includes strong environmental protection.

What You Can Do

There's no end to what you can do once you're at your computer; pick your battles so you won't be overwhelmed. Make a deal with yourself to take at least one action per week (or whatever time period is comfortable). If you're interested in a wide range of causes, pick one and concentrate on that for a predetermined amount of time—a month, for example. Then move on to a new topic. Or if you prefer, choose a different topic each time and see what excites you.

Postings on the various forums will alert you to actions you can take, give you the necessary information, and direct you where to send a fax or E-mail. They may include products to boycott, people to vote for, and letters to write. Share this information with friends.

Chapter 11

Green Computing

C omputers are wonderful tools for positive action, but they also have their negative impact on the environment, during their manufacture, use, and disposal. Here's what you can do to decrease that impact.

Action 33

Computer Napping and Other Ways to Save Energy

On average, computers use only as much energy as an incandescent lightbulb. Yet because of the sheer number of computers in use (more than 148 million worldwide), 5 percent of U.S. commercial energy is needed just to power them, and the percentage is climbing.

Computers don't need to consume nearly as much energy as they do, and the Environmental Protection Agency has initiated a program to reduce their energy draw. Called Energy Star, the

Sources for this section include: Lester Brown et al., *The State of the World* (New York: Norton, 1994); Kelly S. Betts, "The Coming Green Computers," *E Magazine*, March/April, and "Notes," May/June 1994 (*E Magazine* is a publication of Earth Action Network, Norwalk, CT).

program encourages computer manufacturers to offer models that use less energy than their forerunners and also have a feature that puts the computer to sleep when it isn't in use; this sleep function effectively reduces energy consumption to almost nothing during downtime. The EPA estimates that by the year 2000 energy savings could reach 26 billion kilowatts—the amount of electricity currently consumed in Vermont, Maine, and New Hampshire each year. Reducing energy use will also reduce air pollution by an estimated 20 million tons of carbon dioxide, 140,000 tons of sulfur dioxide, and 75,000 tons of nitrogen oxide.

What You Can Do

If you're in the market for a new computer, contact the EPA at 401 M St., SW, Washington, DC 20460; (202) 233-9114, for a complete list of manufacturers offering models that meet Energy Star criteria, or ask your local dealer. Many of the new energy-saving models have additional environmentally friendly features, like plastic parts coded for recycling, that your dealer should be able to tell you about.

If you already own a personal computer, retrofitting may be the way to go. There are a number of products on the market that can be plugged into your current model to create the energy-saving sleep function. Ask your dealer.

To achieve the greatest efficiency for the least amount of money, get into the habit of turning off your computer, printer, and desk lamp whenever you aren't using them, and encourage friends and coworkers to do the same.

Action 34
Using Fewer Trees to Save the World

The dream of a paperless office brought about by the computer age has failed to materialize. In fact, we're using more paper than ever. However, a new generation of equipment and business practices may help reduce the paper glut. For example, more than eighteen thousand organizations in the United States now bypass paper in favor of electronic data interchange for exchanging invoices, purchase orders, and other information.

What You Can Do

Try to print out documents on recycled paper and advocate for the recycling of office paper in your community.

Some newer printers allow double-sided printing. If you, or your company, are in the market for a new printer, look into these. (Many new printers also tend to use less toner and electricity.)

To reduce paper use further, get into the habit of doing more editing and proofreading on-screen. You may reduce your own paper consumption dramatically by not printing out so many revisions.

If the computers in your office are connected by a network, encourage everyone to create an electronic "in box" for memos, announcements, and other forms of office correspondence.

Action 35

Using Recycled Computer Disks

Every year software publishers pull hundreds of thousands of unsold boxes of software programs from the shelves to make way for new, improved versions. And what becomes of the old boxes, filled with unused disks? Many vanish into the counterfeit software business and many more end up at the dump. Up to 30 million disks are wasted this way every year. The GreenDisk Company now recycles some of these unsold disks, which are "cleaned" to be as good as new, and sells them for 10 percent less than the price of new disks at computer software stores.

What You Can Do

Look for recycled disks at your local computer store. If you can't find recycled disks on the shelf, ask if the store could carry them.

For more information, contact GreenDisk, 15530 Woodinville-Redmond Rd., Suite 400, P.O. Box 1546, Woodinville, WA 98072-1546; (202) 489-2550.

Action 36

New Homes for Old Computers

As computers become able to process more information more quickly, it's not surprising that consumers are giving up old models in favor of new ones. Unfortunately, demand for older machines is not keeping up with supply, and good equipment is landing in the trash. A study by Carnegie-Mellon University estimates that by the year 2005, as many as 150 million PCs may be filling 300 million cubic feet of space in landfills.

The United States has almost half the computers in the world, with 265 machines per 1,000 people, compared to 57 per 1,000 in Italy and 1 per 1,000 in India and China. It is vital that we deal with disposal issues before the problem escalates. Apple, IBM, and other U.S. companies are now following the lead of European and Japanese manufacturers and have opened facilities to collect old computers. They are also designing new models that are easier to recycle.

What You Can Do

Before you trash an old computer, check with local schools and nonprofit groups—they might love to take it off your hands. Or check with your dealer to see if it will take it back, or contact one of the following organizations, all of which can find good uses for working computers.

EastWest Development Foundation
49 Temple Place
Boston, MA 02111
(617) 542-1234

Educational Assistance Limited
P.O. Box 3021

Glen Ellyn, IL 60138
(709) 690-0010

National Cristina Foundation
42 Hillcrest Dr.
Pelham Manor, NY 10803
(800) 274-7846 or (914) 738-7494

Action 37

Cleaning Up Silicon Valley

Despite its reputation for being a "clean" industry, high-tech electronics manufacturers are contributing an alarming amount of pollution to our environment. You might be shocked to learn that Silicon Valley has one of the highest concentrations of Superfund sites in the country; twenty-eight of the twenty-nine sites in the area are associated with the manufacturing of electronics.

The industry is starting to clean up its act, slowly, thanks to the outcry of people living in communities where electronics manufacturers are concentrated. Citizens' groups in California, New Mexico, Texas, and other areas have formed the Campaign for Responsible Technology to raise awareness of these issues on a national level.

What You Can Do

To learn more about how citizens are fighting to clean up their communities and the electronics industry, contact the Silicon Valley Toxics Coalition, 760 N. 1st St., San Jose, CA 95112; (408) 287-6707.

Part IV

Protecting the Environment

What you can do today to help solve problems ranging from our solid waste crisis to the accumulation of toxins in the environment, while you shop, bathe, travel to work—even while you read this book

Chapter 12

Cleaning Up the Environment Starts at Home

In his 1994 Earth Day speech President Bill Clinton said:

> Since the first Earth Day twenty-four years ago, our nation has been on a journey of national renewal. But as long as 70 million Americans live in communities where the air is dangerous to breathe; as long as half our rivers, our lakes and our streams are too polluted for fishing and swimming; as long as people in the poorest communities face terrible hazards from lead paint to toxic waste dumps; as long as people around the world are driven from their homelands because what were their fields are now deserts, their fisheries are dying and their children are stricken by diseases, our journey is far from finished.

Indeed, our journey to clean up the environment is far from finished. Concentrations of carbon dioxide continue to build in the atmosphere, raising fears about global warming; every year 2.7 billion pounds of toxins are released, legally, into the air we breathe; the hole in the ozone layer is growing; and garbage washes up on the nation's most pristine shorelines.

Around the world, as forests shrink and deserts grow, as water supplies become scarcer and more polluted, people are experi-

85

encing the reality that our life-support system is fragile and has a breaking point. Will the wars of the future be fought over freshwater, firewood, and fertile land instead of for political and ideological reasons? Very possibly, if we all don't contribute to the momentum behind the current environmental movement.

Individuals are now more empowered than they were even a few years ago. Recycling programs are more plentiful and more accessible in urban communities. Cans of dolphin-safe tuna line the shelves of grocery stores. Grassroots environmental groups are gaining support across the country. We all deserve a collective pat on the back, but there is no time to rest on our laurels. Each of us needs to continue the good fight in a hundred little ways, from the time we get up in the morning and remember to turn off the water while we brush our teeth to the time we turn off our energy-saving lightbulb and call it a day.

The actions in this section may be second nature for many people. But they are well worth repeating. A refresher course may be just the thing to reinspire you to do more than ever. For others, the information we've included here may be eye-opening, and the actions an exciting way to combat the feelings of helplessness that too much bad news can bring on. In either case, these actions are intended to encourage you to incorporate as many as you can into your daily routine—to make the world a better place for all of us.

Chapter 13

Rain Forest Protection

Action 38
Saving the Rain Forests

All of the plants, animals, insects, and other life forms that pop-
ulate our earth are intricately connected in a complex web that
has evolved, slowly, over millions of years. No one can say what
damage is done by the destruction of one fine strand, but in the
course of every hour of every day we destroy over 4,000 acres of
rain forest, and every day of every year we permanently wipe
out close to 50 different species of plants and animals. As the
forests are destroyed, so are the cultures and lives of the people
who live there.

In the past thirty-five years, more than 50 percent of the
earth's rain forests have been destroyed. Environmentalists fear
that in another thirty years, there may not be any tropical forests
left. What about life on earth after the rain forests are gone?
Stanford University biologist Paul Ehrlich warns: "We are
destroying a part of the planet's heritage that is crucial to our
health, to our climate, to the very maintenance of our biosphere.
Second only to nuclear war, there are few problems more criti-

Sources for this action include Scott Lewis, *The Rainforest Book* (New York:
Berkley Publishing, 1993).

cal to humanity at the moment." But the destruction continues; on average, 67 acres of rain forest are demolished each minute and an area larger than the size of a football field is destroyed every second of every day. A million species of plants and animals will be extinct by the turn of the century.

The decline in tropical forests is due, in part, to consumer demand in industrialized countries. The United States, for example, obtains much of its timber from tropical forests. Each year logging removes about 12,000 square miles of these forests. Meanwhile, reforestation is proceeding very slowly in the tropics. In many places, ten trees are cut for each one planted; in Africa, twenty-nine trees are cut for each one planted. The developed world's consumption of tropical hardwoods has increased fifteen times since 1950; consumption in tropical countries has increased only three times. As loggers selectively fell commercially valuable tree species—which sometimes account for less than 5 percent of the trees in any given hectare (2.47 acres)—they often destroy 30 to 60 percent of the unwanted trees at the same time.

The clearing of tropical forests for cattle pasture is another reason for the decline of these areas. For example, the growing imports of beef to the United States from southern Mexico and Central America during the past thirty years have been a major factor in the loss of about half of the tropical forests in those areas—all for the sake of keeping the price of a hamburger in the United States about a nickel less than it would be otherwise.

Population growth, inequitable land distribution, and the expansion of export agriculture have greatly reduced the area of cropland available for subsistence farming, forcing many peasants to clear virgin rain forests. These displaced cultivators often follow traditions of continuous cropping that are ill suited to fragile forest soils. Eventually the soils become so depleted that peasant colonists must clear more forest to survive, a cycle that continues over and over. Another factor is the relentless search for fuelwood. Nearly 1.5 billion people—one-third of the world's population—are cutting firewood, often their only source of heat and energy, faster than the wood can be regrown.

In the United States, the tropical forests on Hawaii, Puerto Rico, the U.S. Virgin Islands, and American Samoa are also being destroyed by urbanization, recreational development, and geothermal power and hydropower projects.

Tropical rain forests play a critical role in our everyday lives and are essential to continued human survival on the planet—often in ways we are unaware of or take for granted.

1. We use *tropical rain forest* products when we read a book, drive a car, drink coffee, apply deodorant, eat chocolate, or take a pill. The list of industrial, medicinal, and agricultural uses is long and impressive.

2. More than one-quarter of the pharmaceuticals prescribed in the United States are derived from *tropical rain forest* plants. The rosy periwinkle of Madagascar contains alkaloids that have revolutionized the treatment of leukemia and Hodgkin's disease. Seventy percent of plants identified as having anticancer properties are native to *tropical rain forests*.

3. Tropical deforestation will severely affect the global climate. Rain forests, as do all forests, consume carbon dioxide through photosynthesis, counteracting the greenhouse effect of the carbon dioxide we pump into the environment. Without these forests to slow global warming, Siberia may soon become the world's breadbasket and New York City a place that only scuba divers visit. Because plants also *store* carbon, burning the rain forests releases large quantities of carbon into the atmosphere, accelerating the greenhouse effect.

4. Tropical deforestation affects short-term global weather conditions as well. The absence of huge areas of tree cover causes more sunlight to be reflected off the earth's surface, disrupting wind currents and rainfall patterns. Additionally, as the rain forests' sponge effect (their ability to absorb and recirculate rainfall) is lost, floods and droughts become exaggerated, leading to massive soil erosion on the one hand and desertification on the other.

What You Can Do

1. U.S.-based timber corporations are still active in tropical deforestation. American consumers spend upwards of $2 billion a year for tropical hardwood products. Furniture imports account for more than $1 billion worth of U.S. trade. Another $1 billion is spent to import semimanufactured products such as panels, plywood, veneer, and joiners (for use in the construction of floors, windows, shelves, counters, and so on).

   To learn more about the best wood products to buy, consult Rainforest Alliance's "Smartwood Certification Program," 65 Bleecker St, New York, NY 10012-2420; (212) 677-1900.

2. Ask before you buy. Don't purchase tropical wildlife like parrots and macaws, or tropical plants like orchids and bromeliads, unless you can be sure they have been raised or grown in the United States rather than taken from the wild.

3. Encourage local merchants who sell furniture and beef products to find out where their products come from. If they come from tropical forests or land that was once forest, don't buy them.

4. Communicate your views on saving tropical forests to the agencies and development banks that provide loans to tropical countries. Write to: President, World Bank, 1818 H St., NW, Washington, DC 20433; Administrator, U.S. Agency for International Development, 2201 East St., NW, Washington, DC 20520; and President, Inter-American Development Bank, 1300 New York Ave., NW, Washington, DC 20577.

5. Look for people and organizations in your community that may already be involved in saving tropical forests, and join in their work (the conservation groups listed in Action 39 can help you).

6. Purchase products that are sustainably harvested from the tropical forest, such as Rainforest Crunch products from

Community Products, Inc., in Montpelier, Vermont; (802) 229-1840, and skin-care products from the Body Shop's mail order catalog; (800) 541-2535. Many natural foods stores also carry personal care and other products that contain sustainably harvested rain forest ingredients.

7. Adopt an acre of rain forest from the Nature Conservancy, or become a guardian of the Amazon through the World Wildlife Fund. For $35 the Nature Conservancy will send you an honorary land deed and will use your money to purchase and conserve tracts of the rain forest. For $25 the World Wildlife Fund will set aside land, hire local people to protect it, and teach others how to harvest the forest's bounty sustainably. For more information, write Adopt-an-Acre Program, The Nature Conservancy, 1815 N. Lynn St., Arlington, VA 22209, or World Wildlife Fund, 1250 24th St., NW, Washington, DC 20037.

Action 39

Sources of Rain Forest Information and Actions

Conservation International, is reachable at 1015 18th St., NW, Suite 1000, Washington, DC 20036; (202) 429-5660.

Cultural Survival, Inc., which publishes *Cultural Survival Quarterly,* is at 46 Brattle St., Cambridge, MA 02138; (617) 621-3818.

Rainforest Action Network publishes the *World Rainforest Report* and *RANAlert* for all members contributing $15 or more at 450 Sansome St., Suite 700, San Francisco, CA 94111; (415) 398-4404.

Rainforest Alliance, 65 Bleecker St., 6th Floor, New York, NY 10012; telephone: (212) 677-1900; fax: (212) 677-2187, publishes *The Canopy,* a quarterly, and *Hot Topics from the Tropics,* a bimonthly newsletter for all members contributing $25 or more. Both are excellent publications, covering international developments, research reports, book reviews, and a calendar of events. For those interested in supporting beneficial rain forest legislation, the "Capital Briefs" column in *The Canopy* will be of special interest.

The Rainforest Foundation, 270 Lafayette St., Suite 1205, New York, NY 10012; (212) 431-9098, focuses its attention primarily in Brazil, where it has succeeded in demarcating a portion of the rain forest roughly the size of Switzerland. It has funded many programs ranging from health care to education. Contact the foundation for additional information, to make a contribution, or to request a copy of its quarterly newsletter.

Chapter 14

Solving Our Transportation Dilemma

Action 40
Automobiles—the Bane of Urban Life

Automobiles and trucks are responsible for 30 percent of the nation's carbon dioxide emissions, a major cause of acid rain and the greenhouse effect. Two-thirds of the land in the city of Los Angeles is devoted to highways, roads and parking lots. Our nation's thirst for gasoline has left traces of oil from spills and accidents that can be found in every body of salt water on the face of the planet.*

Industrial cities typically relinquish at least a third or more of their land to roads and parking lots. In the United States, this totals in excess of 38 million acres—more than the entire state of Georgia.

Traffic congestion is eroding the quality of life in urban areas,

Sources for this action include: Lester R. Brown et al., *State of the World: A Worldwatch Institute Report on Progress toward a Sustainable Society* (New York: Norton, 1994). For more information about the Worldwatch Institute, contact it at 1776 Massachusetts Ave., NW, Washington, DC 20036; (202) 452-1999. "The Second Coming of the American Small Town," *Wilson Quarterly* (Winter 1992).
*Excerpted with permission from Marcia D. Lowe, "Pedaling into the Future," *World Watch* magazine, July/Aug. 1988.

and the amount of time wasted in traffic continues to expand in the world's cities. London's rush-hour traffic crawls at an average of 8 miles an hour. In Los Angeles, motorists cumulatively waste 100,000 hours a day in traffic jams. Traffic engineers estimate that by the turn of the century Californians will lose almost 2 million hours daily.

Emissions from gasoline and diesel fuel use are linked to as many as 30,000 deaths annually in the United States alone, and some 100,000 people in North America, Western Europe, Japan, and Australia died in traffic accidents in 1985. Developing countries—with fewer automobiles but more pedestrian traffic and no provisions for separating the two—have fatality rates as much as twenty times higher than industrial countries.

In 1950 there was 1 car for every 46 people worldwide; currently there is 1 for every 12 people. In the United States the figure jumps to 1 car for every 2 people. The average American household makes about 5 trips a day, covering an average of 37 miles: 13 miles from home to work (roundtrip), 5 miles to go shopping, 8 miles on personal business, and 11 miles to take the children to ballet lessons, go to the health club, and socialize with friends. Dependence on the automobile is exacerbated by poor planning, which results in increased driving. Suburban sprawl in Orlando, Florida, has increased the number of household trips to 13 per day.

What You Can Do

1. Minimize the use of your automobile by walking, bicycling, joining a car pool, or taking public transportation. Transportation is now the largest and most rapidly growing drain on the world's oil reserves. The United States uses fully 65 percent of its oil in transportation, more than the country produces.

2. If you must drive, use a fuel-efficient car. Already there are several models on the road that achieve over 50 miles per gallon. Prototypes are in development for models that will go up to 100 miles per gallon. The key factor to

remember is that if you switch from a car that gets 25 miles to the gallon to one that gets 50, you'll cut in half the dangerous emissions you cause every time you drive.

3. Also remember to keep your car tuned up and your tires inflated to the proper pressure; don't use your air conditioning unnecessarily; and when you are on the highway, use cruise control if you have it. All of these actions will save you money on fuel and ensure that your car runs more efficiently.

Action 4!

The Car of the Future

The ideal "green" car of the future will consume no fossil fuels and generate no pollution, the car itself will consume fewer resources during the manufacturing process, and it will be easily disposed of.

The first step toward the creation of such a car is the electric vehicle. Electric motors have negligible direct emissions and are quiet and efficient and draw no power when stopped. In addition, electric vehicles can take advantage of regenerative braking, which allows them to recover energy normally lost through friction. Regenerative braking is even more significant today, since more and more driving is done in congested, stop-and-go conditions.

Electric cars are not as complex as gasoline-powered cars, so they require less maintenance. The total cost of operating a traditional gasoline-powered vehicle over 100,000 miles is $0.22 per mile, $0.15 of which is for maintenance, whereas an electric vehicle averages $0.08 per mile with only $0.03 for maintenance.

Recharging the battery of an electric car with electricity generated from coal results in some emissions, but large power plants tend to be more efficient and less polluting than small internal combustion engines. Electricity generated by renewable energy sources—wind, water, and solar—produces almost no pollution.

Air pollution standards adopted by California, New York,

and Massachusetts require that "zero-emission" vehicles, such as electric cars (the other zero-emission car in development is powered by a hydrogen fuel cell), make up 2 percent of the cars sold in 1998 and 10 percent of those sold in 2003. The big three automakers are developing electric vehicles. General Motors has developed the Impact, a car that is pollution-free and quiet, uses one-fifth as much energy from fossil fuels as gas-fueled cars, and has a recyclable battery pack. It plans to release the car in 1995. Several smaller companies have electric and even some solar-assisted cars available now. Check out the electric vehicle directory in the following list of resources.

The next generation of zero-emission cars will be hybrid cars that combine the advantages of electric motors with the advantages of storing energy in chemical fuels. Using a gasoline engine to drive small electric motors that power the wheels, the hybrid maximizes the engine's efficiency by allowing it to operate at a steady speed even during acceleration and deceleration. Amory Lovins of the Rocky Mountain Institute, a leading promoter of energy-efficient technologies, believes these cars can achieve fuel efficiencies of 150–250 miles per gallon. Made of lightweight composite materials, they have superior aerodynamics, highly efficient tires, and fuel cells to generate the necessary electricity.

What You Can Do

1. Buy, construct, use, or support the development of electric, hybrid, and solar-powered cars.

Consult these resources:

Convert It, by Mike Brown, is a step-by-step manual for converting a gas car into an electric-powered car. $35 from Real Goods Trading Corporation, (800) 762-7325.

Electric Vehicle Directory, by Philip Terpstra, reviews over twenty vehicles on the market today. Complete with specifications, it also lists sources of other electric vehicles as well as components, associations, and newsletters. $11 from Real Goods, (800) 762-7325.

To learn more about electric vehicles, contact any of these organizations:

Electric Auto Association
(800) 537-2882 (for a recorded message to request information)
(510) 685-7580 (to speak to a live person)

Electric Vehicle Industry Association
P.O. Box 59
Maynard, MA 01754-0059
(508) 897-9393
It can tell you where to buy an electric vehicle in your area.

Northeast Sustainable Energy Association
23 Ames St.
Greenfield, MA 01301
(413) 774-6051

Solar Energy Industries Association (SEIA)
122 C St., NW, 4th Floor
Washington, DC 20001
(202) 383-2600

Action 42

The Incredible Bicycle

Traffic noise in Beijing means the whirring of bicycle wheels and tinkling of bells. The streets of New Delhi come alive with thousands of bicycle commuters each day. Office workers in New York City depend on bicycle messengers to cruise past bumper-to-bumper traffic and deliver parcels on time.

Outside the city, bicycles also play a vital role. Kenyan dairy farmers with milk deliveries cycle through remote regions, and Nicaraguan health workers on bikes now reach four times as many rural patients as they did on foot.

Whether a cycle rickshaw in Jakarta or a ten-speed bike

in Boston, pedal power plays a key role in transportation. The bicycle is fast becoming the only way to move quickly through congested urban traffic and the only affordable personal transport in the developing world—where an automobile may cost more than a worker earns in a decade.

Planning Makes a Difference

Like the United States, most other industrial countries have all but abandoned the bicycle for the automobile. Suburbanization has caused jobs, homes, and services to sprawl over such long distances that automobiles are less a convenience than a necessity. Only a handful of North American cities have extensive bike paths, and most major cities have become bicycle-proof, their roadways and parking facilities designed with only motor vehicles in mind. There are, however, outstanding models of nationwide bicycle planning in the Netherlands, West Germany, and Japan. Local governments in these countries—spurred by traffic jams and air pollution—are demonstrating how public policy can be used to make cycling a safe and convenient alternative to the car.

The Netherlands has over nine thousand miles of bicycle paths, more than any other country. In some Dutch cities, half of all trips are made by bike. The West German city of Erlangen has completed a network of paths covering one hundred miles, about half the length of the city's streets. Bicycle use has more than doubled as a result. So many Japanese commuters bicycle to train stations, where they then ride public transportation to work, that the stations need parking towers. The city of Kasukabe now has a twelve-story structure that uses cranes to park more than 1,500 bicycles.*

*Excerpted with permission from Marcia D. Lowe, "Pedaling into the Future," *World Watch* magazine, July/Aug. 1988.

In 1991, the U.S. Congress passed and the president signed into law the Intermodal Surface Transportation Efficiency Act requiring states to develop transportation plans and programs that include pedestrian walkways and bicycle transportation. This law also allows flexible funding to provide new federal highway dollars for construction and improvements in pedestrian, bicycle, and mass transit programs.

What You Can Do

Although government must take the responsibility for making roads safe for bicycles, building bike paths, constructing bike parking areas, and conducting safety campaigns—we can all get involved. Retrieve your bike from the cellar or attic, dust it off, oil it, check your tires' air pressure, and pedal every place you can. Pedal for your health, for clean air, for the end of acid rain, and for the hope that our planet will escape the devastating climatic changes that the greenhouse effect could bring our way. The following groups are leaders in advocating programs that encourage the use of bicycles and are working to pass legislation that provides for cyclists' rights:

- ✔ Bicycle Federation of America, 1506 21st St., NW, Suite 200, Washington, DC 20036; telephone: (202) 463-6622; fax: (202) 463-6625. The Bicycle Federation is a national nonprofit organization established to encourage the increased use of the bicycle. It serves as the national clearinghouse for information on bicycling.
- ✔ League of American Bicyclists. This group has been active for more than a century, starting with its campaign for bicycle paths in New York City's Central Park. 190 W. Ostend St., Suite 120, Baltimore MD 21230; telephone: (410) 539-3399; fax: (410) 539-3496.

For additional information on other transportation alternatives, contact any of the following organizations:

✔ American Public Transit Association, 1201 New York Ave., NW, 4th Floor, Washington, DC 20005; telephone: (202) 898-4000; fax: (202) 898-4070. This organization works to promote greater use of public transit. It also works to increase the investment in and availability of public transportation.

✔ Campaign for New Transportation Priorities, 900 2d St., NE, Suite 308, Washington, DC 20002; telephone: (202) 408-8362; fax: (202) 408-8287. This group works on combating problems of congestion, air pollution, energy consumption, and environmental degradation by supporting investments in mass transit, intercity passenger rail, ride-sharing, and bicycle and pedestrian facilities.

✔ National Association of Transit Consumer Organizations, 442 Summit Ave., #2, St. Paul, MN 55102; (612) 227-5171. This national network of transit consumer and advocacy groups was formed to help coordinate the efforts of local groups and to develop support for improved transit services.

✔ Surface Transportation Policy Project, 1400 16th St., NW, Suite 300, Washington, DC 20036; telephone: (202) 939-3470; fax: (202) 939-3475. The STPP is a network of diverse organizations and coalitions whose goal is to develop a national transportation policy that better serves the environmental, social, and economic interests of the nation.

Chapter 15

Saving Energy and Water In and Around Your Home

Home and Appliance: Energy Efficiency and Conservation

Today modern lighting technology could save the United States $30 billion a year, refrigerators exist that use 80 percent less electricity than standard models, and superinsulated homes have been built that need no heating in temperatures down to 40 below zero.

The Problems Are Clear . . .

✔ Our lights, refrigerators, and televisions are powered by electricity from coal-burning generators that spew out the gases that contribute to acid rain and the greenhouse effect.

Sources for this section include: the U.S. Department of Energy, Washington, DC; the American Forestry Association, Washington, DC; L. H. Lovins and A. B. Lovins, *Energy Unbound* (Sierra Club Books); Rocky Mountain Institute (Snowmass, CO); *Garbage*, Spring 1994 (Gloucester, MA); *Greenpeace Magazine*, vol. 13, no. 2.; *World Watch* magazine, May/June 1988, Worldwatch Institute (Washington, DC).

✔ Each year the typical American home is responsible for 25,000 pounds of carbon dioxide and 113 pounds of sulfur dioxide emissions through the direct consumption of electricity and heating fuels.

✔ Most American households waste half the energy they consume through inefficiency, with the average home guzzling 1,253 gallons of oil a year at a cost of $1,123.

... but So Are the Solutions!

✔ If every household in the United States lowered its average heating temperature six degrees for *only twenty-four hours,* more than 570,000 barrels of oil would be saved.

✔ If everyone raised air-conditioning temperatures six degrees, we could save the equivalent of 190,000 barrels of oil every day.

✔ Better yet, if everyone improved home insulation by using the most energy-efficient materials, the same amount of energy would be saved, and no one would even need to touch the thermostat. During the summer, trees properly planted around your home to provide maximum shading could cut your energy bills and use of electricity up to 10 percent by reducing the need for air conditioning.

Energy efficiency saves money and creates jobs. To save the equivalent of 1 kilowatt-hour of energy through conservation would cost one to four cents; this compares favorably to the average cost of producing a kilowatt of energy, which is about six cents. One million dollars spent on energy efficiency will directly create fifty jobs. The same million dollars spent on the petroleum industry will create only ten jobs. That means money invested in saving energy creates 40 percent more employment than the same numbers of dollars spent on creating new energy.

The extraordinary levels of efficiency possible today can be seen in Scandinavia, Canada, and the northern Great Plains of the United States, where Bigelow Homes of Chicago builds new homes guaranteed to get through the winter with no more than

$200 worth of heat per season. This is achieved through designs that take full advantage of the sun's heat, together with superinsulation and airtightness. These superinsulated homes, first developed in Sweden, have walls and ceilings that are insulated to twice the standard level, and the entire structure is protected by a barrier that is extremely effective at blocking wind. So thermally sound are these houses that most of the heating actually comes from occupants, lights, and appliances. Indeed, until recently it was difficult to find furnaces small enough to meet their minuscule heating demands.

But let's not get carried away—we're not all ready to build or buy new homes. Let's simply start with a careful look at our appliances and some other less expensive but effective ways to conserve energy. Since the 1973 oil embargo, homeowners and businesses have cut the nation's energy bills by $275 billion per year through increased efficiency.

Action 43

Energy-Efficient Lighting and Appliances

Residential appliances and heating and cooling equipment consume about one-third of the total electricity produced in the United States. When it comes to saving energy, these are the appliances to focus on. Aside from your central heating system, the following are likely to be the biggest energy users in your home:

Water heater
Refrigerator/freezer
Stand-alone freezer
Air conditioner
Range
Clothes washer
Clothes dryer
Dishwasher
Portable space heaters
Lights

Although many appliance models may look the same, they can be very different when it comes to energy cost. That's why it pays to look closely at energy efficiency. For example, refrigerators that have the refrigerator and the freezer side by side use *35 percent more* energy than models with the freezer on top. Models with manual defrost use *50 percent less* electricity than those with automatic defrost.

Compact fluorescent lightbulbs can provide huge environmental benefits because they use up to 75 percent less electricity than regular incandescent bulbs and they last up to ten times longer. Using a compact fluorescent will slow global warming and reduce acid rain by cutting down on emissions from a typical U.S. coal plant of one ton of carbon dioxide and about 20 pounds of sodium dioxide. If the electricity is being drawn from a nuclear power plant, use of a fluorescent will help avoid the production of half a curie of strontium 90 and cesium 137 (two high-level waste components) and about 25 milligrams of plutonium—nearly equivalent in explosive power to 850 pounds of TNT and sufficiently radiotoxic, if uniformly distributed into the lungs, to cause cancer in about two thousand people.

Compact fluorescents will also save you money, especially now that many utilities offer bulbs at little or no cost to encourage their use. Even if you pay full price, the bulb will cost you less than using the equivalent number of incandescent bulbs because of the energy you'll save.

What You Can Do

1. Before you purchase a new appliance, consult these two booklets from the American Council for an Energy-Efficient Economy: *The Most Energy-Efficient Appliances* covers all the highest-rated models available in the United States and costs $3 (plus $2 for handling). *The Consumer Guide to Home Energy Savings* ($6.95, plus $2 handling) provides additional guidance for the purchase and use of energy-efficient appliances. Both are available from ACEE Publications Office, 2140 Shattuck Ave., Suite

202, Berkeley, CA 94704; telephone: (510) 549-9914; fax: (510) 549-9984.

2. If you're serious about saving the environment by drastically cutting your energy consumption, consider a Sun Frost refrigerator, which uses 80 percent less electricity than the average model. Consider these facts: Most consumers spend $1,000 on a refrigerator, an additional $120 to $180 annually for electricity, or a total of roughly $4,000 over the machine's twenty-year lifetime. The Sun Frost, at a cost of about $2,000, will save more than 75 percent of your energy expenses, or $3,000 worth of electricity over the appliance's lifetime. You can receive more information about the Sun Frost refrigerator from P.O. Box 1101, Arcata, CA 95591; (707) 822-9095.

3. Consider replacing your electric hot water heater if you've got one; gas and oil heaters are generally at least 40 percent more efficient. In addition, almost all hot water tanks waste an average of 20 to 30 percent of the electricity they consume—keeping water hot when it's not needed. This can be minimized by wrapping insulation around the tank and around all hot water pipes. Better yet, "demand-type" water heaters come on only when you turn on the tap—there's no tank, and a high-powered gas burner or electric heating element heats the water only as it is used.

4. No matter what type of water heater you currently own, set the thermostat to "low." For each reduction of 10 degrees Fahrenheit on the dial, you'll save roughly 3 to 5 percent on your heating bill. A setting of 110 degrees Fahrenheit will provide you with water that is more than adequately hot. Also remember to turn off your water heater if you leave home for the weekend or take a vacation.

5. Contact Lehman Hardware and Appliances for its outstanding catalog, which offers hundreds of nonelectric household appliances. Send $2 to One Lehman Circle, P.O. Box 41, Kidron, OH 44636-0041; (216) 857-5757.

6. Order compact fluorescent bulbs from Seventh Genera-

tion's "Products for a Healthy Planet" catalog, 49 Hercules Drive, Colchester, VT 05446; (800) 456-1177; or from Real Goods Trading Corporation, 966 Mazzoni St., Ukiah, CA 95482; (800) 762-7325. Commercial or industrial users, contact: Rising Sun Enterprises, Inc., 40 Sunset Dr., Basalt, CO 81621; telephone: (303) 927-8051; fax: (303) 927-3635.

Action 44

Weatherproofing and Insulation

Every year about $150 worth of energy per household escapes through the holes and cracks in residential buildings. A typical house has enough cracks, leaks, and holes to be equivalent to a three-foot-by-three-foot hole in the wall of the living room. Not much help when you're trying to keep cool in the summer or warm in the winter. A basic weatherproofing program, consisting of weather-stripping windows and doors, tuning up the furnace, and adding some insulation to the attic, can make a big dent in your utility bills and would be a major step toward reducing our overall energy needs.

Windows are a particularly key area of energy loss; as much energy leaks through American windows every year as flows through the Alaskan pipeline. A 50-cent investment in weather-stripping and caulking can save you $5 a winter. Storm windows can double a window's insulating value. If you have south-facing windows, opening the blinds during the day in the winter means your house will soak up the solar heating equivalent of seven gallons of oil. Unfortunately, unless you close the blinds at night, you'll lose just about all the heat you've gained.

A "retrofitting" renovation of your whole house, while expensive, can make an even larger difference. In 40,000 retrofits monitored by U.S. utilities, overall energy consumption fell by 25 percent, and homeowners got a 23 percent annual return on their investment.

If you start from scratch, a superinsulated house that adds several thousand dollars in construction costs, or $35 a month to your mortgage bill, can save an average of $79 a month in utility costs. That's a savings of at least $528 every year, which may increase as the cost of energy rises.

What You Can Do

1. Contact your state energy office or local utility company, or check the yellow pages to find out who will do a free comprehensive energy audit of your home.
2. Your local hardware store probably stocks everything you need to cover windows and doors with plastic sealers that will shrink to fit snugly, as well as liquid caulk, outlet covers, draft stoppers for the bottom of doors, and pipe insulation for hot water pipes. More than enough to get you started.
3. To order a complete line of weatherproofing products by mail, call Resource Conservation at (800) 243-2862; request free samples as well as a copy of its catalog.

Action 45
Solar Energy

The sun can provide many of our energy needs without the devastating side effects caused by fossil fuels, such as acid rain and global warming, and solar energy is renewable and environmentally sound. Converting any part of your energy consumption from electric, gas, or oil to solar power is admittedly much more expensive, involved, and time-consuming than caulking windows or resetting thermostats. However, no discussion of energy conservation would be complete without the introduction of at least one "renewable" energy source. Oil, gas, and coal are considered "nonrenewable" sources, since as soon as you extract them from the earth, they're gone. But the sun is not diminished in its strength or value by our increasingly diverse uses of it.

Solar heating has been around for years. In 1897, 30 percent of the houses in Pasadena, California, used excellent solar water heaters. Today solar technology is so advanced that even in climates having almost constant cloud cover you can still utilize solar heating to turn cool water into steam. Commercially available solar collectors can heat water to as high as 2,600 degrees Fahrenheit. But America is running well behind in its use of solar technology; solar-heated water is used in 12 percent of Japan's homes, 65 percent of Israel's, and 90 percent of Cyprus's. Many of these systems are so simple that they cost only $500 per family to install. And technology is constantly improving; current innovations, which should reach the market by the year 2000, will dramatically reduce up-front costs and increase efficiency.

Today, in addition to heating water and your entire home by the sun, you can purchase solar rechargeable batteries, solar-powered Walkmans, flashlights, fans, and even a solar barbecue. In the Mojave Desert, a private plant owned by Solar Energy Generating Systems supplies enough power for ten thousand homes. Perhaps most important, solar power doesn't pollute our air.

What You Can Do

1. Call or write Rodale Press, 33 E. Minor St., Emmaus, PA 18098; (610) 967-5171, for a copy of its book catalog, which contains a number of excellent do-it-yourself guides. In addition, contact the Rocky Mountain Institute for its publications list: Rocky Mountain Institute, 1739 Snowmass Creek Rd., Snowmass, CO 81654-9199; telephone: (303) 927-3851; fax (303) 927-4178.
2. Real Goods Trading Corporation offers a full range of solar-oriented products. For a free catalog, contact it at 966 Mazzoni St., Ukiah, CA 95482; (800) 762-7325.
3. For more information, contact any of these organizations:

American Solar Energy Society
2400 Central Ave., G1
Boulder, CO 80301

(303) 443-3130
A great resource for anyone interested in solar energy.

Backwoods Solar Electric Systems
8530 Rapid Lightning Creek Rd.
Sandpoint, ID 83864
Telephone: (208) 263-4290
Fax: (208) 265-4788
A great place to go for help designing your own independent energy systems (if you are not connected to public utilities). It offers free consulting and a free catalog of all necessary components for hydro, wind, and solar electric power.

Home Power Magazine
P.O. Box 520
Ashland, OR 97520
(916) 475-3179
Published six times a year ($15 a year or $30 for first-class delivery), this magazine has great information for anyone interested in powering a home with solar-, hydro-, or wind-generated energy.

Solar Energy Industries Association (SEIA)
122 C St., NW, 4th Floor
Washington, DC 20001
Telephone: (202) 383-2600
Fax: (202) 383-2670
Ask for the free publications catalog.

At the same address you can write to the following organizations: National Bio-Energy Industries Association, (202) 383-2540; American Wind Energy Association, (202) 383-2500; and National Hydropower Association, (202) 383-2530.
The Solar Energy Research and Education Foundation specializes in on-line information. Anyone with access to E-mail can access its database on solar power at: serefinfo@crest.org.

Action 46

Energy Conservation Resources

In addition to the resources listed in actions 43, 44, and 45, the following resources can help you discover new ways to save energy:

The Alliance to Save Energy
1725 K St., NW
Suite 509
Washington, DC 20006
Telephone: (202) 857-0666
Fax: (202) 331-9588

Energy Efficiency and Renewable Energy Clearinghouse
P.O. Box 3048
Merrifield, VA 22116
Telephone: (800) DOE-EREC / (800) 363-3732
Fax: (703) 903-9750
Funded by the U.S. Department of Energy, the clearinghouse provides information and technical assistance on energy efficiency and renewable energy technology and offers more than 250 free publications on related topics.

Water Is the Medium of Life

Life on earth began in the water. Today some water is unsafe to drink, let alone fit to create new life. Bathers at beaches throughout the world have to dodge sewage, hypodermic needles, tampons, and poisoned fish. Fishermen haul in sea life complete with cancerous tumors and deadly lesions.

Eighty percent of the weight of a typical living cell is water; ninety-nine out of every one hundred molecules in your body are water molecules. Trace for a moment the path of one of these water molecules. Yesterday, a bit of water may have entered your body as you bit into a tomato; before that, it was part of an oak leaf decomposing in the soil of your vegetable garden. To become that oak leaf, the water molecule surged up the oak tree from its roots, where it was first deposited by a raccoon that had drunk from a nearby pond.

Through water we are connected to the oak, the raccoon, the marsh grass, to clouds and rivers, to soil and oceans. Through water, we are intimately connected to each other and to our entire planet. There is almost nothing that we do that does not affect or rely on water, either directly or indirectly. Every time you press the brake pedal on your car a small amount of asbestos brake lining falls to the street and is later washed by rain into a nearby stream. The product you buy in New Hampshire today was perhaps created in a sulfur-dioxide–spewing factory in Ohio last week; the acid fumes released from this factory may come down as rain in your favorite fishing spot tomorrow. And the half-used box of pesticides you toss into the trash today may leach from the town landfill into your drinking water next year.

Although each of us, on the average, uses about 150 gallons a day directly for cooking, washing, flushing, and watering, our indirect use of water amounts to an astounding 1,840 gallons per day. Of this, about 1,660 gallons are used to grow the crops and livestock we eat, and 180 gallons are used by industry to create products.

Approximately 120 gallons are used in the production of just one egg, three gallons to process one can of corn, ten gallons to make a paperback book, and five to flush a toilet. While new water-saving toilets use as little as 1.5 gallons, most homes still have older, less efficient models that use five or more gallons per flush.

Each time we flush the toilet, those five gallons affect

one or more aquatic ecosystems. If your water comes from a surface reservoir, it was diverted from its downstream course by damming a river, which concentrated pollutants and decreased the oxygen levels necessary for life. Similarly, if those five gallons were removed from underground aquifers their use could ultimately lower the water level in area ponds and lakes.

What happens to the five-gallon flush after it leaves the toilet bowl? If the septic system is malfunctioning, or if there are too many such systems in an area of poor soils, the wastes could seep into ground water and affect the water you and your neighbors use to wash with and drink. If you live in a sewered area, the waste-laden five gallons travel to a waste-water treatment plant, where it may flow untreated into a bay, river, or ocean.

Between 1972 and 1981, under the auspices of the Federal Water Pollution Control Act, we spent over $32 billion in an attempt to make all the nation's waterways suitable for fishing and swimming by 1983. Thirty-seven states did not reach that goal, and the General Accounting Office reported that it doubted whether we can afford to complete the job. It is not surprising that this monumental clean-up effort has been at best a partial success. For while laws, good planning, and funding all help, they will never be enough until we, as a people, learn an ethic of responsible use.*

As usual, ecology and economics speak with one voice. When we conserve water in the home, we save money and aquatic ecosystems. When we maintain our septic systems, we help avoid the need for building expensive new sewage treatment plants that almost always degrade water quality. When we use conservation technologies to water lawns, gardens, and fields, we cut our water bills and reduce the likelihood of damming yet

*Excerpted with permission from the New Alchemy Institute.

another river. When we take action in our communities to influence water supply and water quality planning, we inform our government officials about how much we care about saving money and our ecosystems.

Today there are numerous ways to cut daily water consumption by more than 50 percent without any modification to our comfort or change in our lifestyles. What follows is a description of the simplest, most effective ways to start reducing water usage.

Action 47

The Art of Flushing, Showering, and Bathing

At 5 gallons a flush, with an average of 19 gallons per person a day, and about 7,000 gallons a year, flushing the toilet uses more water than anything else in your household.

At 12 gallons a minute, a two-minute shower uses 24 gallons of water and a ten-minute shower over 100, with the average bath consuming 40 gallons of water. The first thing you can do is keep your shower short and avoid taking baths unless the water level in the tub is kept as low as possible. Low-flow showerheads can cut water use as much as 75 percent by reducing the water flow from 12 gallons a minute to 3. These showerheads still deliver water with invigorating force because of their unique design.

What You Can Do

1. Install state-of-the-art, low-flow toilets, which use only 1 to 1 1/2 gallons per flush, saving as much as 5,600 gallons a year per person. Check with your local dealers for their most efficient models.
2. Both Seventh Generation, (800) 456-1177, and Real Goods Trading Corporation, (800) 762-7325, offer water-saving showerheads that fit easily in any shower without requiring special tools or installation.
3. A complete range of other water conservation products is

available from Niagra Conservation Corporation, (800) 831-8383.

Action 48

Brushing, Shaving, Doing the Dishes, and Washing the Clothes

With the tap running, brushing your teeth can use up to 2 gallons of water, a shave 5–10 gallons, and washing dishes by hand up to 20 gallons.

Most washing machines waste over 5,304 gallons of water every year.

What You Can Do

1. Don't let the tap run while you brush, shave, or scrub. This alone can cut water consumption by 75 percent. Single-lever on/off switches make shutting off the water easier, and they don't waste water because there's no need to adjust for the right temperature when you turn the water back on.

2. Faucet aerators with on/off switches create further savings by reducing the flow from the tap by 60 percent and saving over 6,000 gallons of water every year. Check with your local hardware store or call Real Goods Trading Corporation, (800) 762-7325, or Niagra Products, (800) 831-8383.

3. Front-loading washing machines, used widely in European countries, consume one-third less water (and two-thirds less soap) than conventional top loaders. The ASKO model can save 12,000 gallons a year, which will also save money on the water-heating portion of your energy bills. The ASKO dishwasher is 50 percent more efficient than the average machine available in the United States and 40 percent more energy-efficient. For more information, contact ASKO at (800) 367-2444.

Action 49

Keeping Your Grass Greener

Outdoor water can account for 50 percent of the total amount of water used during June, July, and August. Unfortunately, because of inefficient watering, much evaporates before plants can use it.

What You Can Do

1. Test the soil for dryness by digging a small hole, about 2 inches deep. Water your lawn only when it is dry 1 1/2 inches below the surface. While the grass may look wilted, if there is sufficient moisture in the ground, it is in no danger of dying.

2. If you must water the lawn, do it in the early morning (before 9:00 A.M.) to prevent the sun from evaporating much of the sprinkler's efforts and to prevent wasting hundreds of gallons of water over the course of the year.

3. Mulch your plants with woodchips, pebbles, or hay. This will reduce natural moisture loss and prevent weed growth.

4. Use a drip irrigation system in your garden. For more information, contact Gardener's Supply Company, 128 Intervale Rd., Burlington, VT 05401; (802) 863-1700 or (800) 944-2250.

Action 50

Gray Water Recycling

If you are building a new home or renovating an older one, consider installing a gray water recycling system. These systems can cut indoor water use by a third. The system takes water that has already been used in the shower, bathtub, bathroom sink, washing machine, and kitchen sink and allows its reuse in your toilet or, in the case of shower and sink water, in your garden. Since these systems are not widely used, be sure to have your plans inspected by your local building inspector or health department.

What You Can Do

1. For additional information, order a copy of *Gray Water Use in the Landscape: How to Use Gray Water to Save Your Landscape during Droughts,* a 25-page illustrated guide that shows how to assemble a simple recycling system for your yard and garden. It also includes a list of biodegradable cleaners for your bathroom and laundry which can be used with gray water recycling systems. The guide is available for $6 postpaid from Robert Kourik, Edible Publications, P.O. Box 1841, Santa Rosa, CA 95402.

2. Bi-CEP publishes plans for a gray water recycling system that recycles wash water back into the toilet or out into the garden. The six-page plans are available for $5 postpaid from Lester N. Freed, Bi-CEP, Inc., 20 Indian Valley Lane, Telford, PA 18969.

3. Call or write the U.S. Department of Energy's National Appropriate Technology Assistance Service, P.O. Box 3048, Merrifield, VA 22116; (800) 428-2525.

Chapter 16

Waste Reduction, Recycling, and Composting: Controlling Waste and Consumption

W hen Madison Avenue exhorts us to buy, buy, buy, we may think about the impact on our cash flow, but rarely on the environment. But the truth is that we can't continue to indulge in unbridled consumerism. Denis Hayes, a leading environmentalist, puts it well when he says, "Today's global population cannot ever be sustained at anything approaching the current lifestyles of the United States or Europe or Japan. Since my birth, my fellow Americans and I have consumed more of the world's mineral wealth than all people in all societies throughout the entire course of history before I was born." Has all this consumption brought us happiness? Not according to Hayes. "Study after study has shown that, once a population escapes utter poverty, the correlation between increasing material abundance and happiness is almost random."

All this consumption wastes mind-boggling amounts of raw

Sources for this section include: Lester Brown et al., *State of the World: A Worldwatch Institute Report on Progress toward a Sustainable Society* (New York: Norton, 1994); and William Robinson, *The Solid Waste Handbook* (New York: John Wiley & Sons, 1986).

materials and creates mountains of waste. Every year we throw away: 18 billion disposable diapers, made from 21 million trees; 25 billion Styrofoam cups; over 2 billion disposable razors; 200 million automobile tires; and some 7.5 million TV sets, which if placed in a line would reach from New York to Denver!

Americans throw out fifteen times their weight in trash every year, or about three-quarters of a ton for every person. We throw away enough aluminum to rebuild the entire American airfleet seventy-one times and enough steel to reconstruct Manhattan, and enough wood and paper to heat 5 million homes for two hundred years. Containers and packaging waste account for almost half of this, with 50 percent of the nation's paper, 8 percent of its steel, 75 percent of its glass, 40 percent of its aluminum, and 30 percent of its plastic used solely to package and decorate consumer products.

On a per capita basis, no other country in the world can match our output of garbage. Americans generate 4 to 6 pounds of garbage per day, about double that produced by the typical Japanese, Swiss, West German, or Swedish citizen and almost three times that of the typical resident of Oslo, Norway. The total amount of trash generated in the United States each day— over 600,000 tons—is staggering. It is enough to fill about 60,000 garbage trucks or to load up an armada of 190 ocean-going garbage barges.

Action 51

Throwing Away Our Future: Starting with the Basics

Opportunities to reduce waste present themselves on a minute-by-minute basis, from the moment you rise (and don't use the new pump toothpaste dispenser because of its excessive packaging or shave with a disposable razor) to the moment you go to sleep (putting aside a library book rather than one you bought).

What You Can Do

Reducing waste demands an awareness of:

✔ what you really *need* versus what you *want*
✔ what can be recycled and what can't
✔ what's biodegradable and compostable
✔ how to avoid products that you use once and throw away
✔ what products utilize the least amount of packaging

In addition, the following eight general rules will help you to lead a less wasteful life:

1. Purchase goods packaged in glass, metal, or paper—avoid plastic and Styrofoam, which are not as readily recyclable.
2. Purchase in bulk or family size; besides saving money, you'll reduce the overall amount of packaging you're consuming.
3. Purchase fresh produce from green markets rather than produce that has been packaged for supermarket distribution.
4. Read labels; many companies are now using post-consumer recycled materials for their packaging.
5. Buy durable, long-lasting products. The extra price you pay is usually a bargain when it comes to both quality and reduced waste. *Consumer Reports* magazine—monthly, $22; call (800) 234-1645 or write Consumers Union, 101 Truman Ave., Yonkers, NY 10703—is a good source of information for any major purchase.
6. Borrow before you buy. Don't purchase something you're only likely to use on a rare occasion. Borrow the item from a friend, whether it be a ladder, slide projector, power tool, or toilet plunger. Many power tools and do-it-yourself items are also available for rent. Check the yellow pages for everything from baby furniture to party supplies, electric sanders, and audiovisual equipment.

7. Maintain and repair the products and equipment you own. Don't put off that service call or the purchase of a replacement part. Even shoes last longer if you take care of them.

8. Avoid impulse buying. Don't leave home without a list of what you need, and try to stick to it. If you are unsure that you need something, you probably don't. Shopping is not a cure for loneliness and depression. It leaves you feeling worse when the bills come. Both you and the environment end up poorer.

Action 52

Recycling: Closing the Loop

Recycling works only when the materials we collect as waste are turned back into "raw" materials for manufacturing. If there's no market for recycled materials, they will eventually end up in landfills, despite everyone's best efforts.

A few years ago it was enough to look for products and packaging that were "recycled." Now, with distinctions being made between "pre-consumer" and "post-consumer" recycled materials, it's important to understand the distinction between these two terms.

Post-consumer refers to all the material that passes through consumers' hands on the way to the waste stream. For example, a newspaper that you read and recycled is considered to be post-consumer waste. But a newspaper that languished on the newsstand and was never sold to a consumer before being recycled is not.

Pre-consumer refers to waste that is created during the manufacture of goods (or goods that are recycled without ever having been sold—such as the unwanted newspaper mentioned above). During the printing of your Sunday paper, for example, a certain percentage of paper is wasted when the presses are set up. If this waste paper is recycled, it is considered pre-consumer recycled material.

Federal legislation now requires the disclosure of post-consumer content for any items claiming to be recycled (unfortunately, many companies don't yet comply). If there's no indication of post-consumer content, it's a safe guess that pre-consumer recycled waste was used to make the product.

Not only does closing the loop complete the recycling process and ease the burden on our landfills, but it also saves valuable nonrenewable natural resources. Products manufactured with recycled materials dramatically reduce water and air pollution (see the table below).

What You Can Do

Buy products made from recycled materials whenever possible. Check the packaging for post-consumer content. If you have a choice, select the item with the highest post-consumer content. The Seventh Generation Catalog, (800) 456-1177, has over one hundred products made from post-consumer recycled materials (for more resources, see Action 53).

Environmental Benefits Derived from Substituting Recycled Materials for Virgin Resources

Environmental Benefit	Aluminum	Steel	Paper	Glass
Percent reduction of				
Energy use	90–97	47–74	23–74	4–32
Air pollution	95	85	74	20
Water pollution	97	76	35	–
Mining wastes	–	97	–	80
Water use	–	40	58	50

Source: Robert Cowles Letcher and Mary T. Sheil, "Source Separation and Citizen Recycling," in William D. Robinson, ed., *The Solid Waste Handbook* (New York: John Wiley & Sons, Inc., 1986).

Action 53

Resources for Recycling Information

What You Can Do

The following organizations are all excellent resources for
information about recycling:

Environmental Defense Fund
257 Park Ave. S.
New York, NY 10010
Telephone: (212) 505-2100 or
(800) CALL EDF
Fax: (212) 505-2375

Environmental Protection Agency
401 M St., NW
Washington, DC 20460
(202) 260-6261

Greenpeace USA
1436 U St., NW
Washington, DC 20009
Telephone: (202) 462-1177
Fax: (202) 462-4507

National Recycling Coalition
1101 30th St., NW
Suite 305
Washington, DC 20007
Telephone: (202) 625-6406
Fax: (202) 625-6409

You can also contact your state department of natural
resources or local environmental planning commission.

To order products made from recycled materials, contact these companies for their direct-mail catalogs:

Earth Care
966 Mazzoni St.
Ukiah, CA 95482
(800) 223-4000

New England Cartographics, Inc.
P.O. Box 9369
N. Amherst, MA 01059
(800) 286-4124
(413) 549-4124

Peacetree Recycled Paper
523 NE Davis
Portland, OR 97232
(503) 233-5821

Seventh Generation
49 Hercules Dr.
Colchester, VT 05446-1672
(800) 456-1177

Real Goods Trading Corporation
966 Mazzoni St.
Ukiah, CA 95482
(800) 762-7325

Action 54
Municipal and Home Composting

From 20 to 30 percent of the municipal waste stream is composed of organic kitchen and yard wastes. Many communities are establishing composting programs to reduce the volume of waste landfilled. Yard waste is collected separately from other wastes, then composted into a nutrient-rich mulch and soil conditioner that can be used to slow soil erosion, improve water retention, and increase agricultural yields.

Composting is most advanced in Europe, where special composting facilities speed up the natural breakdown rate by creating an optimal environment for waste decomposition. France alone has more than one hundred plants producing over one million tons of compost each year. In Sweden one-fourth of all solid waste is composted. By the spring of 1993, twenty-two municipal solid waste composting facilities were in operation in the United States. In New Jersey a program of state-sponsored economic incentives has spurred more than eighty municipalities to develop leaf composting and mulch programs. Broome County, New York, banned leaves from its landfill to encourage local townships to establish composting programs. Since 1989 some of the residents of Guelph, Ontario, have been separating their trash into "wet" recyclables, "dry" recyclables, and rubbish. City officials say that a 60 percent recycling rate can be achieved using this type of combination system, with only 4 percent of the trash being placed in the wrong container.

What You Can Do

1. Composting is easy to do in your own backyard. For more information, order "Let It Rot! The Complete Home Gardener's Guide to Composting," from Gardener's Supply Company, 128 Intervale Rd., Burlington, VT 05401; (802) 863-1700. Gardener's Supply also sells a variety of composters.

2. The key to creating a marketable final product from a community composting program is to separate out only the compostable materials.

3. If your community doesn't offer composting, find out why. Call the municipal department that handles solid waste for your area, and start asking questions. Tell the staff you believe municipal composting is an essential part of a sound waste management strategy. Your questions alone may be enough to get some wheels turning in city hall.

4. Even apartment dwellers can compost with worm bins, which silently, odorlessly, and very efficiently turn the food waste of a family of four into rich compost—all inside a little black box that will easily fit below the sink. Available from Seventh Generation, (800) 456-1177—one pound of friendly red worms included. Check with local hardware stores and nurseries for indoor composters, or make one yourself!

Chapter 17

Toxins and the Environment

No information is available on the toxic effects of more than 79 percent of the 48,500 chemicals listed in the EPA inventory. But many of these chemicals are contributing to indoor air pollution, which the EPA tells us is often many times worse than air pollution outdoors. A careful look in the bathroom cabinet, under the sink, and in the basement or garage will explain why. The list of poisonous chemicals found in common household products is long enough to fill a book.

Action 55

Protecting Yourself and the Planet from Toxic Chemicals

Industry, agriculture, and a society determined to clean, disinfect, polish, and deodorize—as well as rid itself forever of the nasty little creatures that we believe are determined to invade our homes—are producing some unhappy results.

Sources for this section include Lester Brown et al., *State of the World: A Worldwatch Institute Report on Progress Toward a Sustainable Society* (New York: Norton, 1994).

✔ Half a million fish were killed when pesticides accidentally spilled into the Rhine River.

✔ Deadly chemicals banned for use in the United States may still pose a threat to consumers in industrial countries, because manufacturers continue to sell them to Third World countries. When industrial countries import food from their poorer neighbors, they end up consuming the same deadly chemicals that have supposedly been banned.

✔ We assault the Third World in more direct ways, too. Soap containing mercuric iodide, whose sale is forbidden in Europe, is sold to African distributors. This soap, used to "lighten the skin," can cause fetal damage, anemia, and renal failure.

✔ Worse, DDT and benzene hexachloride (BHC), both banned in the United States and much of Europe, account for a significant amount of the total pesticide use in India. Residues of these compounds, both suspected carcinogens, were found in all seventy-five samples of breast milk collected from women in India's Punjab region. Through their mothers' milk, babies were daily ingesting twenty-one times the amount of these chemicals considered acceptable. Similarly, samples of breast milk from Nicaraguan women have shown DDT levels that are an astounding forty-five times greater than tolerance limits set by the World Health Organization.

✔ Routine agricultural practice in the United States has contaminated groundwater with more than forty-seven pesticides in twenty-six states.

✔ As many as ten thousand landfills and other waste sites may now cost between $750 billion and $1.5 trillion to clean up—the equivalent of $3,000 to $6,000 for every U.S. resident. Not surprising, since we dump the equivalent of one ton of hazardous waste per person into the ground every year.

Not a pretty picture. Again, the question is, What can we do? Admittedly, most of our planet's toxic problems are caused by industrial agriculture and municipal waste-disposal practices, but a careful look in our homes will reveal that we are willingly, though perhaps unknowingly, bringing many of the most poisonous chemicals right into our homes. The consequences and risks of using many of these chemicals are not even known.

Unfortunately, the toxins that can be found in typical consumer products are so diverse and at times so complex that a complete list can't be presented here. The resource section that follows in Action 56 will direct you to a number of excellent publications and organizations from which you can obtain much more complete and detailed information.

What You Can Do

✔ Don't dispose of hazardous chemicals (such as automotive products, painting supplies, lawn-care products, and cleaning products) by pouring them down the drain or toilet. Carefully follow disposal instructions when dealing with ALL toxic products. Many areas now have special drop-offs for hazardous waste and places to recycle batteries and motor oil. Call your state or local department of waste management for more information.

✔ Avoid buying toxic products if at all possible, and search for nontoxic substitutes to do the same job.

✔ If you must purchase a toxin, do so in the smallest possible quantity.

Action 56

Hazardous Household Products

Do you have any of the following products in your home: disinfectants, furniture polish, bleach, floor wax, drain cleaners, silver polish, rug cleaners, spot removers, paint thinner, car wax, or mothballs?

Most people have them all, and unfortunately each and every one is likely to contain toxic chemicals that are hazardous to the environment and contribute to indoor air pollution. Worse yet, this list of dangerous products is far from complete.

What You Can Do

1. The most constructive actions we can take as consumers start with replacing toxic substances with nontoxic alternatives. Consult the book *Clean and Green: The Complete Guide to Nontoxic and Environmentally Safe Housekeeping,* by Annie Berthold-Bond (Woodstock, NY: Ceres Press), for hundreds of nontoxic cleaning tips and do-it-yourself cleaner recipes.
2. Switch to vegetable-based cleaning products. Seventh Generation, Ecover, and a number of other companies market environmentally friendly ways to do your laundry, clean the bathroom, and get dishes sparkling clean. You'll find a wide selection in most natural foods stores and some grocery stores.
3. Most paints, stains, and thinners are highly toxic and major contributors to indoor air pollution. Oil-based paints are the worst. Latex paints are less toxic. If you are currently storing paint in your house, try to move it to a shed or garage. Better yet, donate it to a school or organization that could use it right away. For future painting projects, consider some of the nontoxic vegetable-based paints and stains that are on the market. They tend to be more expensive than oil-based paints, but they work well, without harmful side effects. The following companies offer paints, stains, and other environmentally friendly household products. Call them for complete listings.

Eco Design Company
1365 Rufina Circle
Santa Fe, NM 87505
(505) 438-3448

Healthful Hardware Catalog
P.O. Box 3217
Prescott, AZ 86302
(602) 445-8225

Simply Better, the Environmental Store
90 Church St.
Burlington, VT 05401
(802) 658-7770

4. The Household Hazardous Waste Project publishes one
of the best resources for nontoxic alternatives to dangerous household products and a detailed review of which
toxins are in most household products. Its *Guide to
Hazardous Products around the Home* is available for $9.95
from 1031 E. Battlefield, Suite 214, Springfield, MO
65807; (417) 889-5000. The book also contains disposal
guidelines, product-labeling information, and many other
valuable tips.

Action 57

Testing Your Home for Toxins

A wide variety of toxins can contaminate the air you breathe,
the water you drink, and even the dishes you use. Radon, an
odorless, colorless, potentially lethal gas, may be seeping into
your house through the foundation. The water coming out of
your tap may not be as pure as you think it is, and the new set
of plates you just bought may contain unacceptably high levels
of lead. The only way to know for sure is to do some testing.

What You Can Do

1. Test your water. Home kits are available to test tap water
for contaminants ranging from bacteria to lead. Check
your local hardware store or natural foods store or contact:

Healthful Hardware
P.O. Box 3217
Prescott, AZ 86302
(602) 445-8225

SelfCare Catalog
5850 Shellmound Ave.
Suite 390
Emeryville, CA 94662
(800) 345-3371

2. Test for radon. It's impossible to predict where radon seepage will occur; it could be a problem for just one house in an entire neighborhood. Radon levels are highest nearest to the foundation, so while it's a good idea for every household to do a radon test, it is especially important for anyone who sleeps or works in a basement, lives in a house that has no basement, or lives in a superinsulated house. Tests need to be sent to a lab for results (included in the price of your kit). The resources listed above can help you.

3. Test your microwave oven and other electrical equipment. Microwave leakage is dangerous to your health and not uncommon in older ovens. Electromagnetic radiation has been linked to a weakening of the immune system and other health problems; test appliances for excessively high levels. Also check bedrooms that are near power lines; avoid electric blankets and other electric appliances near sleeping areas. Handheld meters are made for these types of tests. Available from the SelfCare and Healthful Hardware catalogs (listed above).

4. Test your dishware. Despite federal regulations, high levels of lead and cadmium have been found in glazed dishware, such as bone china and pottery, made by leading manufacturers—a $1,000 place setting from Tiffany's was discovered to have one hundred times the amount of lead allowed by the law. Simple tests for lead are available in

hardware stores and from sources such as those listed above ("What You Can Do #1") that give you an instant reading of lead content (if lead is not present, cadmium is not likely to be a problem). If your dishes do have high lead content, or if you're in the market for new dishes, invest in a set of 100 percent lead-free, cadmium-free dishware. Available from Seventh Generation, (800) 456-1177, and other sources.

Chapter 18

Pesticides

Toxic pesticides (the general term for such poisons as insecticides, herbicides, rodenticides, and fungicides) ultimately touch everyone's life. We are exposed daily to pesticides in the workplace, in the water we drink, through community and household spray programs, or as neighbors of dump sites and sprayed fields and forests. While the chemical industry pushes these "wonder drugs," medical problems with long-term repercussions have already begun to develop.

Myths of Safety

Myth 1: A pesticide is safe because it is registered by the U.S. Environmental Protection Agency and your state.
Myth 2: A pesticide is safe when it is used according to product label instructions.

At the heart of any discussion of pesticide safety is the status of what we know and do not know about the pesticide product in   question. While we may know something about the effects of one chemical, we may know almost nothing about another. In fact, a 1982 U.S. Congressional staff report indicates that: (i) between 79 and 84 percent of pesticides on the market have not been adequately tested for their capacity to cause cancer; (ii) between 90 and 93 percent of pesticides have not been adequately tested for their ability to cause genetic damage; and (iii) between 60 and 70 percent have not been fully tested for their ability to cause birth defects.*

There are three main areas where we are most likely to use pesticides: (1) in our homes to kill bugs, flies, mosquitoes, spiders, and ants; (2) in our gardens to protect flowers, vegetables, trees, and plants; and (3) on our lawns. Consumer pesticide use is no small matter, amounting to a total of over sixty-five million pounds of toxic nonagricultural chemicals a year.

Action 58

What You Can Do in the Garden

Organic gardening—that is, gardening without the use of toxic pesticides and chemical fertilizers—has long been established as an effective, economical, and environmentally sound way to grow vegetables, trees, bushes, and flowers. There are numerous resource providers, including catalog companies like the Necessary Trading Company and Gardener's Supply Company. Both catalogs sell almost everything imaginable for organic and environmentally sensitive gardening, from soil-testing equipment and services to composts and fertilizers, potting soil, disease control formulas, insect traps, and lawn-care equipment.

What You Can Do

The Necessary Trading Company Catalog is also full of educational information, how-to publications, and a list of relevant books. For a free catalog, write P.O. Box 305, New Castle, VA 24127, or call (703) 864-5103.

*Excerpted with permission from "Pesticide Safety" by the National Coalition against the Misuse of Pesticides, Washington, DC.

The Gardener's Supply Company catalog is also full of a wide range of terrific products. Call (802) 863-1700, or write to 128 Intervale Road, Burlington, VT 05401.

Rodale Press is an excellent source of how-to information with an extensive list of books and magazines, including Rodale's *Organic Gardening*. To order the magazine, write P.O. Box 7320, Red Oak, Iowa 51591, or call (800) 666-2206 or (215) 967-5171. Subscriptions are $25 for one year.

Action 59

Nontoxic Lawn Care

In 1987 eight million American homeowners spent over $1.5 billion to have chemical companies provide them with perfectly green lawns. The thirty to forty different pesticides used by these companies, such as ChemLawn, an industry leader, can kill birds and endanger our water supply. They have proven to be a formidable threat to children, dogs, and the occasional adult who unsuspectingly wanders onto a freshly sprayed lawn. When sprayed, the chemicals also become airborne and can drift to affect neighbors.

What You Can Do

Nontoxic lawn maintenance can achieve equally effective results and includes:

✔ planting well-adapted and pest-resistant grass varieties
✔ aerating the lawn regularly
✔ controlling thatch buildup
✔ balancing the lawn's pH level
✔ proper watering
✔ mowing the grass with sharp blades, with the mower set as high as possible

Equally important is avoiding the use of chemicals to kill weeds around the driveway, sidewalk, or deck. The worst and most powerful of these toxins, called systemic weed killers, are designed to seep deep into the soil and kill plants from the roots up. If you're a golfer or live near a public park, you might also inquire about lawn-care practices in these areas and voice your concern if toxins are being used. Consult Rodale Press and the Necessary Trading Company Catalog (see Action 58).

Action 60

Resources for Controlling and Reducing the Use of Toxic Chemicals

1. Citizens Clearinghouse for Hazardous Wastes, Inc. (CCHW), P.O. Box 6806, Falls Church, VA 22040; (703) 237-2249. The Citizens Clearinghouse will endeavor to answer any questions its members have about toxins over a special phone line. It also publishes *Everyone's Backyard,* which focuses on local organizing actions, legal issues, scientific and technical subjects, and news from local groups that are fighting toxic problems in their communities. CCHW also supports the efforts of more than 1,700 grassroots organizations and 400 neighborhood groups by providing technical assistance, research, and educational programs. Membership is $25.

2. Environmental Protection Agency (EPA), (800) 424-9346. The EPA publishes *Household Hazardous Waste,* a free bibliography of useful references and a listing of state experts throughout the country.

3. National Coalition against the Misuse of Pesticides (NCAMP), 701 E St., SE, Suite 200, Washington, DC 20003; telephone: (202) 543-5450; fax: (202) 543-4791. Comprised of three hundred groups plus hundreds of individual members, NCAMP is the primary national organization working on pesticide issues. It promotes public policy reform and provides referrals to local pesticide action groups and other contacts. A staff toxicologist helps answer pesticide questions. The quarterly newsletter, *Pesticides and You,* costs $25, which includes membership.

Practical fact sheets will help you solve almost all your home, garden, and lawn-care problems.

4. Bio-Integral Resource Center (BIRC), P.O. Box 7414, Berkeley, CA 94707; (510) 524-2567. BIRC prescribes integrated pest management (IPM) strategies for controlling pests that attack building structures, plants, or pets. Membership benefits include a detailed written consultation on a pest problem and a subscription to the *IPM Practitioner* or *Common Sense Pest Control Quarterly* for $25. For more details and a catalog of IPM publications and audiovisual materials, send $1 and a self-addressed, stamped envelope to BIRC.

5. Concern, Inc., 1794 Columbia Rd., NW, Washington, DC 20009; telephone: (202) 328-8160; fax: (202) 387-3378. An environmental education organization that publishes concise, readable community action guides on pesticides, hazardous wastes, and ground and drinking water contamination. It also provides answers to and referrals for pesticide questions.

6. Rodale Press, Inc., 33 E. Minor St., Emmaus, PA 18098; (610) 967-5171. Rodale is one of the best resources in the field. For $1, you can receive *Resources for Organic Pest Control,* which includes information on practical steps you can take, a list of organic manufacturers and suppliers, pest control materials you can grow or make yourself, and resources for answering pesticide questions. Ask for a catalog and list of magazines, which will include such excellent publications as *Organic Gardening.*

7. The pesticide hotline of the National Pesticide Telecommunication Network (NPTN): (800) 858-7378. Funded by an EPA grant and located at Texas Tech University, NPTN answers pesticide questions from 8:00 A.M. to 6:00 P.M. central time, Monday through Friday. It provides technical chemical and regulatory information, toxicity and health data, and referrals to residue testing labs, poison-control centers, and local doctors experienced with pesticide poisoning.

Chapter 19

Other Great Stuff You Can Do!

Action 61

Dressing Green: Environmentally Safe Clothing

The manufacturing of textiles—even supposedly "natural" fibers like cotton and wool—is environmentally destructive. Consider cotton: An estimated 50 percent of all pesticides in the U.S. are applied to cotton; many of the pesticides, herbicides, and all fertilizers used to grow cotton are derived from petroleum. Even wool, which comes from sheep, a renewable resource, has its environmental toll. For years, environmentalists have urged sheep farmers in the western states—the source for nearly all U.S. wool—to protect sheep with guard dogs rather than by poisoning or shooting puma, coyote, and other sheep predators.

Synthetics like nylon are made from petroleum derivatives, and are manufactured by companies with poor environmental records. Du Pont, the world's largest synthetic fabric maker, ranks as one of the top U.S. polluters.

Several technological developments have spurred the growth in greener fabrics. Tencel, a new fiber made from wood pulp, is one promising innovation. The fiber is processed from trees grown specifically for clothing manufacture. Esprit's Ecollection is one of the several companies blending Tencel with other fibers for its garments.

Another promising fiber is hemp, a durable, annual plant with large yields per acre. A product of the *cannabis sativa* (marijuana) plant, hemp is grown outside the U.S., so little is known about methods of production.

One of the greatest boons to the green cotton market is Fox Fibre, a naturally colored cotton used by Levi Strauss, Esprit, L. L. Bean, and other companies. The invention of entomologist and yarn spinner Sally Fox, Fox Fibre grows in colors including: caramel brown, sage green, and cream. The colored cotton has many other environmental pluses: it requires no bleaching and fewer pesticides, because it is more resistant to pests.*

What You Can Do

Resources for environmentally friendly textiles:

Earthlings, Fox Fibre organic cotton baby clothes: (805) 646-7770.

Esprit Ecollection Catalog, a line of "socially and environmentally responsible clothing": send your name and mailing information to: Esprit, 900 Minnesota Ave., San Francisco, CA 94107 Attn: Catalog Dept.

O Wear, casual knit clothing from organic cotton: (910) 547-7714.

Seventh Generation, untreated cotton sleepwear, underwear, and linens: (800) 456-1177.

Simply Better, the Environmental Store, offers a selection of hemp and cotton clothing and accessories from a variety of companies: (802) 658-7770.

*Excerpted with permission from Joel Makower, "Behind the Seams: The Budding Crop of Earth-Minded Clothing," *Coop America Quarterly*, Summer 1993.

Hemp clothing and fabric are available from the following:

Acton & Co.: (510) 526-4022
Coalition for Hemp Awareness: (602) 988-9355
Exotic Gifts: (707) 725-9798
Hempcat Production: (414) 964-6685
Ohio Hempery: To order, (800) BUY-HEMP; for information, (614) 662-4367

2. If you're in the market for shoes, check out the offerings from Deja Shoe. The first company to make shoes entirely from recycled, post-consumer materials, it offers a wide selection of footwear ranging from sneakers and hiking boots to ladies' casual dress shoes. Look for them in shoe stores. For more information, contact Deja, Inc., 7165 SW Firloop, Suite 200, Tigard, OR 97223; (503) 624-7443.

Action 62

Support Legislation that Protects Endangered Species

According to a report issued by the Science Advisory Board of the Environmental Protection Agency, habitat alteration through deforestation and soil erosion, species extinction and overall loss of biodiversity are among the greatest threats to the global environment.

Right now there are 1,232 plant and animal species officially listed as "endangered" or "threatened" worldwide. While some species have been hunted to near extinction, most are the victims of pollution and the destruction of the ecosystems where they live and breed.

Human carelessness has caused the problems, and it will take human intervention to alleviate it. In the past two decades the Endangered Species Act has been a powerful tool for protecting biodiversity in the United States. The act provides strict guidelines for protecting plant and animal species that are in danger of extinction. The California gray whale, which at one time was on the verge of dying off, was removed from the endangered/ threatened species list; protection measures helped its population grow from 1,500 to 21,000. However, the California gray whale is one of only six species to have been removed from the list. An inspector general's report stated that thirty-four species went extinct before the U.S. Fish and Wildlife Service could even list them.

What You Can Do

Support legislation, such as the Endangered Species Act, that affects habitat preservation and wildlife protection. To find out what legislation you can take action on right now, contact the National Audubon Society, 666 Pennsylvania Ave., SE, Washington, DC 20003; (202) 547-9009.

Action 63
Keeping Alien Species out of Your Local Habitat

A looming obstacle to both the recovery of endangered species and the preservation of biodiversity is the threat posed by species that have been introduced outside their native habitats. Such species, described as "alien," "exotic," or "feral," are a form of biological pollution. These opportunistic invaders— whether plant, insect, mollusk, bird, snake, mammal, or other— are often aggressive and prolific.

What You Can Do

1. Don't introduce plants, animals, or insects from one ecosystem (local or global) to another. If there are no natural predators or other checks to prevent a population explosion, the introduced species may take over. Starlings

are the perfect example. A few were brought to the United States in the late 1800s by a man who wanted all the birds mentioned in Shakespeare's plays to be represented here. Since then, they have become a nuisance to people and outcompeted other species, like bluebirds, for food and nesting space. Anyone who lives in an area where the prolific kudzu vine is strangling the life out of every other plant in the vicinity can also tell you how disastrous the innocent introduction of an exotic species can be.

Some exotic species are introduced on purpose; others are moved to new environments by unsuspecting carriers. If you are traveling from one locale to another, even within the same state or country, don't bring along flora or fauna that may be native to only that part of the world. When you are traveling abroad, be aware of restrictions regarding the transport of plants and animals, and if you receive a package from another region, check it for bugs that may have crept into the box.

Around the country there are people working to control exotic plants that have become problems and to promote local species. These organizations call themselves Exotic Pest Plant Councils (EPPC), and they would welcome your involvement. Contact the EPPC nearest you:

Exotic Pest Plant Council (EPPC)
c/o Sandra Vardaman
Dade County Dept. of Parks and Recreation
Natural Areas Management
22200 SW 137 Ave.
Goulds, FL 33170

CalEPPC
c/o Sally Davis
448 Bello St.
Pismo Beach, CA 93449

PNWEPPC
4409 SW Obsidian
Redmond, OR 97754

TenEPPC
c/o Brian Bower
4824 Torba Dr.
Nashville, TN 37204

Most states have native plant societies. For a list, contact:

California Native Plant Society
1722 J St.
Sacramento, CA 95814
(916) 447-2677

The 1992 Plant Conservation Directory is available for $15 from:

The Center for Plant Conservation
P.O. Box 299
St. Louis, MO 63166

EcoNet subscribers (see Action 31) can post questions to Steve Harris at sharris@igc.apc.org

Chapter 20

Environmental Action Letters, Phone Calls, Jobs, and Voting

There is probably a bill in Congress that needs your support, whether you want to save wolves, whales, and sea turtles, the air you breathe, and the water you drink; fight new highways; save national parks; outlaw unnecessary packaging; support environmental justice organizations; or control acid rain.

Action 64

Whom to Write to and What to Write About

Writing letters, claims the *Audubon Activist*, "is the single most important thing you can do to influence environmental issues." The magazine offers these letter-writing tips, adapted from *The Right to Write* by former Congressman Morris K. Udall:

✔ *Address it properly.*

Honorable_____   Honorable_____
U.S. House of Representatives   U.S. Senate
Washington, DC 20515   Washington, DC 20510

✔ *Identify the bill or issue.*
✔ *The letter should be timely.*

✔ *Concentrate on your own delegation.* Letters written to congressmen or congresswomen in other districts are simply referred to your own representative.

✔ *Be reasonably brief.* Many congresspeople receive more than 150 letters a day. It is not necessary that letters be typed, have perfect grammar, or be beautifully phrased, only that they be intelligible.

✔ *Ask for a response.* Don't hesitate to ask questions (but don't be demanding or threatening).

✔ *Write your own views, not someone else's.*

✔ *Give your reasons for taking a stand.* Your congressperson may not know how the bill may affect an important segment of his or her constituency.

✔ *Show understanding.* Try to show an awareness of how the proposed legislation would affect not just the environment, but also your community and other people's health and jobs.

✔ *Be constructive.* If you believe a bill takes the wrong approach, offer an alternative. If you have expert knowledge, share it with your elected representatives.

✔ *Use personal or business letterhead whenever possible.* Be sure to include a complete return address.

There are many resources for keeping yourself informed on the status of current legislation. Following are some of the best:

1. The *Audubon Activist* is full of suggestions on how to get involved, and it is in every way an outstanding publication. As a bonus, it's exceptionally well written and designed. Topics for letter writing are suggested in its "Conservation Issue Update" column as well as in special "Action Alert" mailings that members and subscribers receive periodically on certain critical wildlife and wilderness issues. Available from the National Audubon Society, 700 Broadway, New York, NY 10003; (212) 979-3000.

2. *Earth Island Journal* is published quarterly by the Earth Island Institute, 300 Broadway, Suite 28, San Francisco,

CA 94133; (415) 788-3666. The *Journal* is an unusually activist publication with "What You Can Do" notes at the ends of most articles. Earth Island Institute is involved in sponsoring, supporting, or coordinating twenty different projects, ranging from the Japan Environmental Exchange to the Sea Turtle Restoration Project. Several topics are usually covered in great detail in each issue of the journal; there is a strong focus on international environmental issues and many brief news items.

3. *Environmental Action* is a quarterly publication dedicated to providing readers with the resources, background, and latest information they need to be effective activists. From coverage of local issues to national politics, industry trends, and scientific developments, *Environmental Action* is a wonderful resource packed with names, numbers, facts, and ideas. Contact the Environmental Action Foundation at 6930 Carroll Ave., Suite 600, Takoma Park, MD 20912; telephone (301) 891-1100; fax (301) 891-2218.

4. *Garbage: The Independent Environmental Quarterly* covers issues including good plastics versus bad plastics, radon, chlorine, recycling in Europe, alternatives to harmful products, designing your kitchen for recycling, and gardening without pesticides. And on top of all that, there is no advertising to distract you from the issues at hand. *Garbage,* 2 Main St., Gloucester, MA 01930; (800) 274-9909 (to subscribe); (508) 283-3200 (main office).

5. *Greenpeace Newsletter* is dedicated to building environmental awareness and activism for Greenpeace members. The articles focus on legislative as well as corporate issues that are both national and international in scope. Every article is followed by a section titled "What You Can Do" that provides you with the names, addresses, and phone numbers you'll need to make your voice heard. Greenpeace USA, 1436 U St., NW, Washington, DC 20009; (202) 462-1177.

6. The *Amicus Journal,* published quarterly by the Natural Resources Defense Council (NRDC) for its members. The

journal discusses environmental actions of the NRDC as well as those of other organizations. The magazine includes a "Current Legislation" column. For more information contact NRDC, 40 West 20th St., New York, NY 10011; (212) 727-2700.

7. *Friends of the Earth,* the newsletter of Friends of the Earth, is published bimonthly and is free to members. The publication covers the full range of environmental issues with "What You Can Do" suggestions at the ends of most articles. The reporting is very strong and supported by the research and legislative work carried out by Friends of the Earth. Of special interest are its international perspectives, detailed and up-to-date explanations of the issues, and coverage of special topics like labor and the environment. Write or call Friends of the Earth, 1025 Vermont Ave., NW., Washington, DC 20005; (202) 783-7400.

8. *Sierra Club Activist Network* is one of the most sophisticated and effective networks around. Divided into twenty-five areas of specific interest, from air quality to mining law, it can notify you whenever environmental legislation is in need of help. "Action alerts" will fill you in on the background and details of the issue and let you know whom to call or write. To join, contact Campaign Desk, Sierra Club, 730 Polk St., San Francisco, CA 94109; (415) 776-2211.

9. *Everyone's Backyard: The Journal of the Grassroots Movement for Environmental Justice* is put out by the Citizen's Clearinghouse for Hazardous Wastes, Inc. CCHW is an environmental justice center working with over 1,700 local grassroots groups. The clearinghouse formed to help people who were fighting for the cleanup of hazardous waste landfills and demonstrating against proposed ones. Over the years its work has grown to include chemical plants, radioactive waste, medical waste, recycling, and other environmental issues. Its mission is to help people build strong community-based organizations, and it provides organizing and technical assistance through manuals and

handbooks, site visits, and over the phone. Its journal is compiled with the help of hundreds of local contacts, who send in clippings and other information about what is happening in their areas. It is well written and informative. For more information on how to receive the journal or contribute to it, contact: CCHW, P.O. Box 6806, Falls Church, VA 22042; 703-237-2249.

10. *Public Citizen* is published by the nonprofit organization of the same name founded by Ralph Nader, one of the most outspoken and influential environmentalists of our time. The organization lobbies for strong consumer protection laws, and the journal will keep you abreast with these and other issues. For more information, contact Public Citizen, 2000 P St., NW, Suite 610, Washington, DC 20036; (202) 833-3000.

Action 65

Support an Environmental Group

No matter how dedicated you are to caring for the environment, you can't be everywhere at once, following legislation, protecting and restoring rivers, forcing corporate polluters to clean up their act, and so on. But your donations to environmental groups ensure that this work goes on. Without supporters like you, the thousands of people who staff groups around the country wouldn't be able to continue their invaluable efforts. Whether you choose to support one group or many, your contributions will make a big difference. Throughout this section, you'll find the names and addresses of groups that deserve your attention. Below we've included some great groups that aren't listed anywhere else in the book. When you're deciding where to lend your support, don't forget local grassroots organizations that are working to protect the environment in your own community—even a small donation of time or money can make a big difference to their very survival.

American Rivers
801 Pennsylvania Ave., SE

Suite 400
Washington, DC 20003
(202) 547-6900

Center for Marine Conservation
1725 DeSales St., NW
Suite 500
Washington, DC 20036
(202) 429-5609

Clean Water Action
1320 18th St., NW
Suite 300
Washington, DC 20036
(202) 457-1286

Defenders of Wildlife
1101 14th St., NW
Suite 1400
Washington, DC 20005
(202) 682-9400

Institute for Conservation Leadership
2000 P St., NW
Suite 413
Washington, DC 20036
(202) 466-3330

The Land Trust Alliance
1319 F St., NW
Suite 510
Washington, DC 20004
(202) 638-4725

Union of Concerned Scientists
26 Church St.
Cambridge, MA 02238
(617) 547-5552

Zero Population Growth
1400 16th St., NW
Suite 320
Washington, DC 20036
(202) 332-2200

Action 66

Saving the Planet Twenty Minutes at a Time

Do you have twenty minutes a month to get involved with national and international environmental legislation? Twenty minutes are all you need to make a difference. Each month an organization called 20/20 Vision can help you identify the best way to spend twenty minutes to protect the environment and preserve peace. It contacts national and local policy analysts and tailors its recommendations to inform you about your locally and federally elected officials and where they stand on important issues. Each month you'll receive an action postcard with the necessary information for writing a brief letter or making a phone call to key policy makers facing crucial decisions.

On this postcard will be:

✔ Subject: The subject that needs your attention is identified. Subjects include preserving ancient forests, cleaning up national waterways, increasing the use of renewable energy sources, enacting campaign finance reform, stopping the proliferation of all weapons, and strengthening UN peacekeeping efforts.

✔ Background information: You get enough information to take effective action, but not enough to overwhelm you. No mountains of mail. No meetings.

✔ Action: You find out whom to contact, when to do it, and what to communicate to make the most of your twenty minutes a month.

20/20's actions are coordinated to send the right message to the right person at the right time. You will be joined by thousands of 20/20 Vision subscribers to get your message heard. In addition, every six months you will receive an update on the results of your actions.

What You Can Do

For more information or to become a member, write to 20/20 Vision at 1828 Jefferson Place, NW, Washington, DC 20036; or call (800) 669-1792 or (202) 833-2020. An individual can join for only $20 a year; a family or household for $35.

Action 67

Books and Resources

Although there are hundreds of books that deal with environmental action, these are noteworthy and not mentioned elsewhere in this book.

The Greenpeace Guide to Anti-Environmental Organizations, by Carl Deal. Copies of this book are available for $5 plus $2 shipping per order from Odonian Press, Box 32375, Tucson, AZ 85751; (800) 732-5786. This book is designed to help you identify and understand anti-environmental groups that have declared war on every issue environmentalists support. It supplies an overview of their ideologies, strategies, and tactics and tells you where their money comes from.

How to Save a River presents, in a concise and readable format, the wisdom gained from years of river protection campaigns across the United States. The book begins by defining general principles of action, including getting organized, planning a campaign, building public support, and putting a plan into action. It also provides an important overview of the resource issues involved in river protection and suggests sources for further investigation. To order a copy or to become a member of River Network and receive a free copy, contact: River Network, P.O. Box 8787, Portland, OR 97207-8787; (800) 423-6747.

Action 68

Student Activism

Student activism is once again on the rise. In 1993 youths from around the country met in Cincinnati, Ohio, for the first National Environmental Youth Summit. They discussed both national and international environmental problems and held seminars to discuss successful ways to address these issues. In small towns and large cities around the country, young people of all ages and backgrounds are banding together to fight for their environment. There are a few national environmental youth organizations, but most of the successful efforts are local. To find out about youth groups in your area, contact the local YMCA, YWCA, Boys and Girls Clubs, or your neighborhood school. All of these organizations are likely to know about student environmental efforts. Listed below are a few groups that demonstrate the various measures today's youths are taking to ensure that they have a safe, beautiful environment to grow up in and pass on to the next generation.

Detroit Summer
4605 Cass Ave.
Detroit, MI 48201
(313) 832-2904

The first Detroit Summer took place in 1992, when 120 young adults from around the nation convened in Detroit to help rebuild its neglected neighborhoods. The participants, about half of whom were from Detroit, transformed three vacant lots into public parks, restored abandoned houses, planted trees, painted senior citizen housing, picked up trash, painted a multicultural mural, and established an anti-gang organizing project. The projects were geared toward revitalizing communities through grassroots efforts to create cooperative economic structures that build community rather than destroy it. The Detroit Summer participants also took part in marches, discussions, and workshops that emphasized past and present struggles to rebuild the city of Detroit with more humane and sustainable principles. Since 1992, Summer Detroit has brought young people together each summer and is serving as an arena in which today's youths are realizing their power to improve social and environmental change.

El Segundo Youth Environmental Group/Tree Musketeers
233 Main St.
El Segundo, CA 90245
(800) 473-0263

The Tree Musketeers, an organization run by kids, formed in 1987 and has since planted hundreds of trees in its local community. Among other things, participants raise money, contact shade tree commissions, get permission to plant trees, and educate the public about the importance of trees. The Musketeers has a speakers' bureau to bring information about the environment to other youth and adult groups. It also publishes a regular column in one of the local newspapers. In addition to its beautification projects, it has been successful in convincing store owners to carry more environmentally friendly products and has produced a quiz show that focuses on the environment.

Global Rivers Environmental Education Network
    (GREEN)
721 E. Huron
Ann Arbor, MI 48104
Telephone: (313) 761-8142
Fax: (313) 761-4951
E-mail: green@green.org

GREEN originated as a water quality monitoring project in the Great Lakes region in the mid-1980s. Today GREEN has programs involving tens of thousands of students in all 50 states and 125 countries around the world. Each watershed project is unique, and how it develops depends on the goals and situation of the local community. Students investigate the health of their local river by studying its chemical, biological, and physical characteristics, as well as its history. The information and data gathered are used to identify water quality issues, helping students discover how human behavior and other forces affect water quality. Students from around the world are increasing their knowledge of water systems, applying science to their daily lives, taking action against polluters, and beginning to see themselves as vital stewards of the environment. GREEN produces a newsletter that features articles by participants from around the world as well as classroom activity sheets, research news, and updates from GREEN country coordinators. The organization also has a worldwide computer conference on EcoNet that links teachers, students, and citizens who monitor their rivers and has set up a cross-cultural partnership program that links young water testers from different countries and allows them to discuss methodology as well as cultural perspectives. For more information on how to get a program started in your area, contact GREEN at the above address.

Student Environmental Action Coalition (SEAC)
P.O. Box 1168
Chapel Hill, NC 27514
Telephone: (919) 967-4600
Fax: (919) 967-4648

SEAC is a network of students and youth environmental groups on more than 2,200 campuses across the United States. It has connections to similar networks in more than fifty countries around the world. SEAC began in the spring of 1988, when students at the University of North Carolina in Chapel Hill placed a notice in *Greenpeace* magazine asking students to write if they were interested in forming a national network. The response was overwhelming. Through the network, students share information, support one another's work, and learn how to organize effectively. The coalition also emphasizes the importance of highlighting the connections between traditional environmental problems and many of today's social ills. SEAC has created the People of Color Caucus (POCC) within the organization to address the concerns of youths of color and to increase the levels of equity and power that youths of color possess in the quest for environmental and social justice. SEAC publishes a monthly magazine, *Threshold: The Students' Environmental Guide,* a book describing twenty-five successful projects that student environmental groups have carried out, and assorted fact sheets on topics from recycling to trade.

Action 69

Environmental Action Jobs

What You Can Do

If you are looking for a career in the growing environmental field, the following are great resources:

Earth Work
Student Conservation Association, Inc.
P.O. Box 550
Charlestown, NH 03603
Published by the Student Conservation Association, this publication is packed with current listings of environmental job openings, plus career news, feature articles on the environment, and more. Write for more information.

Environmental Career Opportunities
Brubach Publishing Co.
Box 15629
Chevy Chase, MD 20825
Telephone: (301) 986-5545
Fax: (301) 986-0658
Targeted toward environmental professionals, this biweekly publication lists hundreds of career opportunities in the United States and abroad. Call for subscription information.

Action 70

Environmentally Sound Voting

The League of Conservation Voters (LCV) is a political action committee that works at the grassroots and national levels to find, support, and elect candidates to federal office who will vote and sponsor legislation to protect the environment.

The LCV's public education activities include publication of the *National Environmental Scorecard*, the standard by which candidates for federal office are judged on their commitment to environmental protection. The league's board compiles a list of the floor votes, cosponsorships, and letter signatures that are most important to the environmental movement. It rates members of Congress for their records on these issues. The *National Environmental Scorecard* is distributed to members of Congress, the media, and the public at large. The league's other public education activities have focused on grading presidential candidates' records on environmental protection.

What You Can Do

Obtain a copy of the *National Environmental Scorecard* by writing the League of Conservation Voters at 1707 L Street, NW, Suite 550, Washington, DC 20036; (202) 785-VOTE. And, it goes almost without saying, **vote** in the next local, state, or federal election.

Part V

Food, Hunger, and Agriculture

What you can do at your next meal to eat healthier while you protect the environment, feed the hungry in your own neighborhood, help solve the international food crisis, and get legislative results

Chapter 21

Eight Myths about Hunger

Hunger is perhaps the most urgent, compelling, and emotionally charged issue we confront as we explore how to make the world a better place. Hunger haunts us everywhere—outside our homes, in faraway places, in the pages of magazines, in newspapers, on TV, and in strongly phrased fund-raising letters that greet us in the mail:

> In the ten seconds it took you to open and begin to read this letter, four children died from the effects of malnutrition somewhere in the world.
>
> No statistic can express what it's like to see even one child die that way . . . to see a mother sitting hour after hour, leaning her child's body against her own . . . to watch the small, feeble head movements that expend all the energy a youngster has left . . . to see the panic in a dying tot's innocent eyes . . . and then to know in a moment that life is gone.*

*Excerpted with permission from a UNICEF direct mail fund-raising letter, 1994.

159

Before we begin to explore what each of us can do, it's important to examine eight of the most common misconceptions about what does and does not cause hunger. These myths have been unveiled by Frances Moore Lappé and the Institute for Food and Development Policy. Over twenty years ago, Ms. Lappé, in her book *Diet for a Small Planet,* helped the world see how diet is integrally related to hunger as well as to health. In her later work, she has explored how power and powerlessness underlie all of the issues that surround world hunger and food distribution problems.

Hunger: Myth vs. Reality

Hunger is not a myth, but myths keep us from ending hunger. Only by freeing ourselves from the grasp of these widely held beliefs can we understand the root causes of hunger and see how to bring it to an end.

MYTH 1: *There's simply not enough food.*

Myth: With farmland and other food-producing resources stretched to their limits in so much of the world, there's not enough food to go around.

Reality: Abundance, not scarcity, best describes the world's food supply. Enough wheat, rice, and other grains are produced to provide every human being with 3,600 calories a day—enough to make all of us fat.

Virtually every "hungry" country produces enough food for all its people. Redistribution of a tiny fraction of each country's food supply would wipe out hunger. For example, in Indonesia, which has the second greatest number of undernourished people in the world, redistributing a mere 2 percent of the available food would make a healthy life possible for everyone.

"Hunger: Myth vs. Reality" is excerpted with permission from *Hunger Myths & Facts,* produced by Food First, the Institute for Food and Development Policy, Oakland, CA. For more information about Food First, see Action 87.

Many "hungry" countries export more food and other farm products than they import. India, home to over a third of the world's hungry people, not only has mounting surpluses of wheat and rice—currently more than thirty-two million tons—but also ranks as one of the Third World's top agricultural exporters.

Even famine-ridden regions of Africa, hard hit by drought in the 1980s and 1990s, exported more farm products than they imported, including food aid imports. Although food production in many African nations does appear to be declining, the causes are not so much natural limits as human decisions. Most notably, since colonial times government policies have systematically favored production of export crops over local food crops. Being human-made, the causes of Africa's food crisis are reversible.

Here at home scarcity can hardly explain the lack of adequate diet for 30 million Americans—not when overproduction is the American farmer's persistent headache.

In the United States, just as in the Third World, hunger is an outrage because it is profoundly needless.

Hunger is real; scarcity is not.

MYTH 2: *Nature is to blame.*

Myth: Droughts and other disasters beyond human control cause famine.

Reality: Deaths from natural disasters have leaped six-fold since the 1960s, but not because nature has become more cruel. Man-made forces are making more people increasingly vulnerable to nature's vagaries.

Millions live on the brink of disaster because they are deprived of land by the wealthy elite, trapped in the unremitting grip of debt, heavily taxed, or miserably paid. Natural events rarely explain death by starvation; they are the final push over the brink.

Human institutions and policies determine who eats and who starves. In Bangladesh during the 1974 floods, rich farmers hoarded rice to sell for greater profit while famine took 100,000 lives, mostly unemployed landless laborers and their families.

Famines are not natural disasters but social disasters. They result from unjust economic and political arrangements, not from acts of God.

MYTH 3: *There are too many mouths to feed.*

Myth: Hunger is caused by overpopulation. Reducing population growth is the best way to combat hunger.

Reality: Although rapid population growth is a serious concern in many countries, nowhere does population density explain hunger. In India over 300 million people are chronically hungry. Yet neighboring China, with only half the cropland per person of India, has eradicated widespread and severe hunger.

Rapid population growth is not the root cause of hunger. Like hunger itself, it results from underlying inequities that deprive poor people, especially women, of economic opportunity and security. Rapid population growth *and* hunger are endemic to societies where landownership, jobs, education, health care, and old-age security are beyond the reach of most people.

Those Third World societies successful in reducing population growth rates—for example, China, Sri Lanka, and Colombia—confirm that the lives of the poor, especially poor women, must improve before they can choose to have fewer children.

MYTH 4: *We have to choose between food and the environment.*

Myth: Pressured to feed the hungry, we are pushing crop and livestock production into marginal erosion-prone lands, clearing age-old rain forests, and poisoning the environment with pesticides. We cannot both feed the hungry and protect our environment.

Reality: That an environmental crisis is undercutting our food-producing resources and threatening our health is no myth. But efforts to feed the hungry are not causing the crisis.

In many countries, logging and ranching companies are leveling irreplaceable rain forests. The lumber and beef, however, are not for the hungry but for the well-off, often those abroad.

Global pesticide use has expanded from virtually nothing only forty years ago to more than five billion pounds a year.

While the chemical companies would have us believe that pesticides help produce food for the hungry, in the Third World most pesticides are applied to crops for export.

MYTH 5: *The Green Revolution is the answer.*
Myth: Boosting food production through scientific advances is the key to ending hunger.

Reality: In the very countries most touted as Green Revolution success stories—India, Indonesia, Mexico, and the Philippines—production of Green Revolution grains has increased while hunger has worsened.

Throughout much of the Third World today, the widening control of the land by a powerful few deprives nearly one billion rural people of any land at all. And as an Indian farmworker once reminded us, "If you don't own the land, you never get enough to eat, no matter how much it is producing."

Hunger can be alleviated only by redistributing food-producing resources and purchasing power to the hungry.

MYTH 6: *We must increase foreign aid.*
Myth: To help end world hunger, our primary responsibility as U.S. citizens is to increase and improve our government's foreign aid.

Reality: Foreign aid is only as good as the recipient government. The bulk of U.S. aid goes to only a handful of governments; most of them are dead set against reforms that would benefit those in need. Where such governments answer only to elites, our aid not only fails to reach hungry people, but shores up the very forces working against them.

As long as we allow Washington to define the national interest to mean keeping the lid on change in the Third World, our foreign aid cannot help end hunger. We cannot be both against change and for the hungry.

MYTH 7: The free market can end hunger.
Myth: If governments just got out of the way, the market would alleviate hunger.

Reality: The market by definition responds to buying power. It works to alleviate hunger only as the hungry gain more power. A government accountable to all its citizens would actively counter the market tendency toward economic concentration through genuine land, credit, and tax reforms, along with other policies designed to disperse buying power.

Anyone who believes in the usefulness of the market and the urgency of ending hunger should concentrate on promoting not the market but the customers.

MYTH 8: The solution involves sacrifice.

Myth: To end world hunger, Americans would have to sacrifice much of their standard of living.

Reality: The biggest threat to the well-being of the vast majority of Americans is not the advancement but the continued deprivation of the hungry.

Enforced poverty in the Third World jeopardizes U.S. jobs, wages, and working conditions as corporations seek cheaper labor abroad. In a global economy, what American workers have achieved in employment, wage levels, and working conditions can be protected only when working people in *every* country are freed from economic desperation.

As we have seen, because the dispossessed majorities within Third World countries lack buying power, agricultural practices in those countries shift toward growing export crops. These exports further undercut markets for U.S. farmers, and America is made increasingly dependent on the outside world for its food.

What can we do to end hunger now that we better understand what does and does not cause it?

The following section of this book will cover actions you can take at every meal you eat and every time you shop, the importance of eating locally grown organic produce, how the food business endangers human health as well as the planet's, actions to help the hungry, and what you can do about the politics of hunger.

164

Chapter 22

Eat Locally, Act Globally

Most of the agricultural produce that Americans consume is produced by standard commercial agricultural techniques. This system involves the use of chemical fertilizers and petroleum-based pesticides and herbicides. Thus, American commercial agriculture is often a major polluter of the environment, and fertilizer runoff is a major cause of water pollution. Broadcast spraying puts agricultural poisons into the air and water as well as the soil.

In addition, this is not sustainable agriculture. It is steadily destroying the topsoil and the living organisms within. Some observers say that by the turn of the century much of the farmland now in use will be infertile. We may be approaching another "Dust Bowl" era, with disastrous consequences for ourselves and for the rest of the world.

Almost every time we buy a loaf of bread, a can of beans or a head of lettuce, we are supporting this system of agriculture. And while we may oppose industrial polluters on the one hand we're abetting agricultural polluters on the other if we purchase their products on supermarket shelves. While we're concerned about food scarcity in other parts of the world, we may be contributing to an eventual shortage closer to home.*

The alternative to this environmentally destructive scenario is close at hand. The following actions examine how purchasing organic produce—through the mail, in local green markets, or from a food co-op—can make a big difference. We'll also look at growing your own food and at community gardens as ways to help you become a socially responsible eater.

Action 71

Organic Farming: Regenerating the Earth

On the menu tonight are chicken with gentian violet, potatoes à la chlorothalonil, carrots in triflurolin, and, for dessert, grapes with methyl bromide.

Farmers now spend roughly $1 billion on agricultural chemicals each year. Meanwhile, damage from insects, weeds and disease has increased. Pesticides applied to farmland in California's San Joaquin Valley, the nation's richest agricultural region, have seeped into underground reservoirs over a 7,000 square-mile corridor, contaminating the drinking water of one million residents.

Across the country, valuable topsoil is eroding at dangerous rates. Streams are poisoned by chemicals washing off the land. Underground reservoirs are being depleted by farmers irrigating fragile drylands that experts say should not have been farmed at all.

Yet amid this tableau of ecological damage, a dramatic and strategic change in production practices is appearing. Increasingly effective techniques for growing food have been developed that could dramatically change the way farming is done in this country.

---

*Reprinted with permission from _East West: The Journal of National Health and Living_ (now called _Natural Health_, Brookline Village, MA).

From Virginia to Oregon, tens of thousands of farmers have reduced their costs and increased their profits by replacing conventional industrialized farming techniques with sophisticated organic ones. They are not, however, just the backyard gardeners usually associated with back-to-the-land organic movements. They also include some of the biggest farms and some of the large users of petro-chemical pesticides and fertilizers.

This farming method, called *regenerative agriculture,* will not solve such critical farm problems as excessive debt, dwindling export trade, or fluctuations of the dollar over-seas. Yet a growing body of state, federal, and private experts agree that modern organic cultivation practices can restore the natural biological balance to vast stretches of once-depleted farmland while reducing the soil erosion, groundwater depletion and pest damage caused in large part by over-dependence on farm chemicals.*

As consumers, we have a vital role to play in the future direction of agriculture, the survival of organic farms, and the protection of our groundwater, lakes, and rivers. As we learn more about the dangers of the pesticides, waxes, drugs, and preservatives commonly used by the food industry, growing and purchasing organic food become even more compelling actions.

What You Can Do

1. Buy organic food whenever you can. Shop in farmers' markets or natural foods stores, or join a food co-op. Requesting that your local grocery store carry a variety of organic produce is another way to support organic farmers.
2. Write to companies and tell them why you have stopped buying their products. Companies are dependent on sales

---

*Excerpted with permission from Keith Schneider with Dick Russell and Noel Weyrich, "The Re-Greening of America," *New Age Journal,* March 1986.

and are very interested in knowing how consumers feel. Many agribusinesses continue to use pesticides, herbicides, and fungicides because they believe the American consumer wants blemish-free fruits and vegetables. If they learn that what we are truly interested in is healthy food, they will begin to stop using chemicals.

3. There are numerous companies that can supply you with organic products of every sort. Here are just a few.

California Certified Organic Farmers Promotes organic agriculture and certifies organic growers and processors in California. It has a growers list, a certification handbook, and a retail/wholesale guide available. 303 Potrero St., #51, Santa Cruz, CA 95060; (408) 423-2263.

Fiddler's Green Farm A certified organic family farm producing freshly stone-ground baking mixes, hot cereals, granolas, jams, gift packs, and other farm products. Free catalog. RR 1, Box 656, Belfast, ME 04915; (800) 729-7935 or (207) 338-3568.

GEM Cultures GEM Cultures carries cultures to make fermented foods like tempeh, miso, and sourdough bread; it also carries bulk items and gourmet foods. Free catalog. 30301 Sherwood Rd., Fort Bragg, CA 95437; (707) 964-2922.

Gold Mine Natural Food Company Organic and wild foods: hard-to-find grains, beans, macrobiotic specialties, books, and eco-friendly household products. Free catalog. 3419 Hancock St., San Diego, CA 92110; (800) 475-3663.

Krueger-Norton Maple Farm Enjoy pure Vermont maple syrup organically produced on a family farm using alternative energy sources. P.O. Box 363, Cuttingsville, VT 05738; (802) 492-3653.

The Organic Coffee Company, Inc. This certified organic coffee roaster offers a wide selection of unique blends. Donations are made to grassroots environmental groups in both coffee-producing and coffee-consuming areas. 12 Kendrick Rd., #7, Wareham, MA 02571; (800) 758-5282.

Walnut Acres One of the oldest and largest mail-order

sources for organic food offers bulk items, including grain and flour, and processed items, such as soup, cereal, jam, and vitamins. Free catalog. Penns Creek, PA 17862; (800) 433-3998.

Action 72

Farmers' Markets: Revitalizing Local Agriculture

Tired of long, quiet, narrow supermarket aisles; of produce packed in plastic, frozen into briquettes, or caked with wax? Depressed by the sight of those sad, tired, droopy heads of lettuce; rock-hard, anemic-looking tomatoes; or apples that glare back at you under the hum of fluorescent lights? If you are, then farmers' markets are definitely what you're looking for.

The New York City Green Market, one of thousands across the nation, provides a direct outlet for about 170 farmers from four states who sell fruits, vegetables, flowers, homemade baked goods, dairy products, eggs, herbs, and wines. The majority of the produce sold at the green market is harvested the day before it's sold, and the market is likely to include more than 350 varieties of fruits and vegetables. Prices during the peak season can be 30 percent less than that of produce found in supermarkets.

Shopping at farmers' markets helps revitalize local agriculture, save family farms, and boost production of organic produce. A recent study of Stockton, California, farmers by the California Department of Food and Agriculture showed that while consumers saved money at farmers' markets, farmers earned a 52 percent greater return on produce sold directly to consumers than they obtained by selling to middlemen in the commercial marketing system. These markets also allowed farmers to sell an average of 22 percent of their total crop that would otherwise have gone to waste, since it would have failed to meet sizing, container, and labeling requirements for commercial sale. This is perfectly good food that supermarkets might reject for a minor blemish.

The Texas Department of Agriculture has assisted in the

opening of farmers' markets in over seventy cities. These markets earn the three thousand participating farmers more than $25 million annually.

Since small family farms are the major producers of organic food, are more likely to treat their animals humanely and their land with respect, and are a critical part of our nation's heritage and economic stability, shopping in farmers' markets does help to make the world a much better place.

What You Can Do

Shop in your local farmers' market. The "calendar" section of your local paper will probably have a listing of when and where farmers' markets are happening near you, or call your state department of agriculture or local chamber of commerce for information.

Action 73

The New York–L.A. Broccoli Shuffle

In one year New York area residents buy approximately 24,000 tons of broccoli—importing almost all of it from the West Coast, nearly 2,700 miles away. The cost: $6 million for transportation alone.

What's more, refrigerated broccoli loses 19 percent of its vitamin C in 24 hours, 34 percent in two days.

The absurdity is this: Broccoli prefers cool weather and could have been grown at home, providing additional jobs and income for New York residents.

Robert Rodale, publisher of *Prevention* magazine, and founder of the Cornucopia Project, says, *"For every two dollars we spend to grow food, we spend another dollar to move it around.* Not just to New York. *Massachusetts imports more than 80 percent of its food, and Pennsylvania—a leading agricultural state in the U.S.—more than 70 percent."*

Here are some startling facts that turned up in the Cornucopia report: "New Yorkers spend approximately

$1 billion a year on food transportation. New York State imports 77 percent of its celery, 95 percent of its pork, 84 percent of its lettuce, 93 percent of its peaches, 97 percent of its chicken, and 87 percent of its green peppers. This is a typical example of what goes on in other states. And consider that the cost of shipping one truckload of greens from California averages $2,400 today.*

Local economies suffer, family farmers go out of business, the quality of the food we eat declines, and our environment suffers as huge corporate farms burden the earth with massive amounts of pesticides and careless farming techniques that cause tremendous soil erosion.

What You Can Do

Eat a "local diet." Doing so will create jobs in your geographic region, keep money in the community, reduce transportation costs and energy consumption, ensure higher nutritional value, and encourage local small-scale agriculture that protects land from developers.

Another great way to enjoy local produce is to get involved in a community-supported agriculture project (CSA). CSAs are large vegetable gardens that are financed by community members, who also, in many cases, contribute a nominal number of hours to weeding and other chores. The payoff is a bounty of inexpensive, freshly grown vegetables. For more information, contact one of the following groups:

AgAccess
P.O. Box 2008
Davis, CA 95617
(800) 235-7177
AgAccess publishes Healthy Harvest IV: Directory of Sustainable Agriculture and Horticulture Organizations.

*Excerpted with permission from *The Tarrytown Letter,* Sept. 1984.

Perhaps the most comprehensive listing of sustainable agriculture organizations, this book describes over six hundred organizations, indexed by subject and geographic region. AgAccess also has a free catalog of agricultural and horticultural books.

Bio-Dynamic Farming and Gardening Association
P.O. Box 550
Kimberton, PA 19442
(800) 516-7797 or (215) 935-7797
The association is the national clearinghouse for community-supported agriculture and bio-dynamic gardening (an organic growing method that emphasizes low environmental impact and biological harmony). It has a database of over four hundred CSAs and bio-dynamic gardening groups, and it publishes a free brochure entitled Introduction to Community-Supported Farms and Farm-Supported Communities. *Call for a listing of CSA and bio-dynamic gardens in your area.*

Community Supported Agriculture of North America
c/o Robyn Van En
Route 3, Box 85
Great Barrington, MA 01230
Publishes information on how to start a CSA project in your community. Send a stamped, self-addressed for its resource list.

Farm Aid
P.O. Box 228
Champaign, IL 61824
(800) FARM AID
Farm Aid supports strong rural communities, safe food, and healthy environments and is dedicated to ensuring that small family farms continue to exist.

Harvest Times
P.O. Box 127
Mt. Tremper, NY 12457
(914) 688-5030

> *This international newsletter serves farmers and consumers linked through community-supported agriculture, which creates strong local economies and builds communities while growing organic food.*

Action 74

Joining Your Local Food Co-op

Another way to support local agriculture, purchase a vast array of organic produce, and avoid the New York–L.A. broccoli shuffle is to join a buying club or food co-op.

According to Paul Hazen of the National Cooperative Business Association, there are roughly four thousand food co-ops and buying clubs in the United States. About 80 percent of them carry organic produce, and their prices are likely to be 5 to 30 percent less than at traditional supermarkets. Many co-ops depend on the volunteer labor of their members, so in some cases you'll have to pitch in and help out for a few hours a month.

Don't worry; you won't have to compromise variety. North East Co-ops in Vermont, for example, supplies regional food co-ops with a selection of more than 1,300 items, including a full line of dairy products.

What You Can Do

1. Join your local food co-op. For the name and address of the one closest to you, check the yellow pages or contact the National Cooperative Business Association, 1401 New York Ave., NW, Suite 1100, Washington, DC 20005; (800) 636-6222. It has listings of many food cooperatives and is ready to help. It publishes a national directory of more than twenty thousand kinds of co-ops for $4.95 and a free publications catalog that lists over one hundred books and publications about co-operatives. It also has an information package on food cooperatives that contains the book *Starting Out Tight: Guideline to Organizing a New*

Retail Club and the video *How to Start a Cooperative Food Buying Club.*

2. Order *Cooperative Grocer,* a bimonthly magazine for and about food cooperatives. For a free sample issue, write P.O. Box 597, Athens, OH 45701; telephone: (800) 878-7333 or (614) 592-1912; fax: (614) 594-4504.

Action 75

Grow Your Own

Growing your own food, while not a solution for everyone, is one way to eat organic products that are environmentally sound and untainted by social injustice.

The suburbs have the ideal ratio between humans and land for permaculture, a land-use system designed to feed a family on a small plot of land while protecting the environment. *Amateur gardeners can routinely produce four to six times the yield per square foot of professional farmers because of the close attention they can give their plants.* Your backyard just may be America's future breadbasket.

Today 53 *percent of the households in the United States garden. Using only about six hundred square feet on the average, they produce 18 percent of the food in this country.* As a social institution, the lawn originated as a petty imitation of the grand parks of the landed English gentry. To own a bit of park was to be a little bit noble. Food was not produced on the lawn, for that implied an embarrassing need to provide for oneself.

Today, in the United States, there are thirty million acres of lawn—a patch of grass equivalent in area to the state of Indiana. This amounts to about one twelfth the area of all U.S. farmland. Almost all these lawns are watered, and they consume significant amounts of other agricultural materials. For example, the phosphate used on American lawns each year is equal to about one third of that used to grow food for the population of India.

Why not redesign these lawns as small farms? Since they

are irrigated, we should be able to at least double the national yield if edible crops were planted. Thus, we could produce 100 percent of the American food supply, with ample capacity for raising small animals like rabbits and poultry (including their eggs) at most suburban and rural homes.*

What You Can Do

Turn your lawn into a breadbasket; grow your own food. The following sources can help you get started with information and gardening supplies.

Gardener's Supply Company
A Vermont-based national mail-order catalog selling quality gardening equipment, composting supplies, organic fertilizers, pest controls, irrigation systems, greenhouses, and lots more. Promotes sustainable agriculture and organic gardening solutions. Free catalog. 128 Intervale Rd., Burlington, VT 05401; (802) 863-1700.

Johnny's Selected Seeds
Vegetable- and flower-seed breeders, growers, and merchants since 1973. Operates an organic farm and supports organic growers, both home garden and commercial. Free catalog. Foss Hill Rd., Albion, ME 04910; (207) 437-9294.

Mail Order Association of Nurseries
Contact this organization for a directory that describes members and how to get their catalogs. P.O. Box 2129, Columbia, MD 21041; (410) 730-9713.

Nature's Control
Supplier of beneficial insects for home gardeners and garden stores. P.O. Box 35, Medford, OR 97501; (503) 899-8318.

Necessary Trading Company
Also known as Necessary Organics. Carries a range of organic

---

*Excerpted with permission from *Whole Life* magazine, March 1984.

gardening products, including organic fertilizers and pest controls, composting supplies, and a series of books and videos. Free catalog. P.O. Box 305, New Castle, VA 24127; (703) 864-5103.

Nitron Industries

Leading manufacturer of 100 percent organic fertilizers, enzymes, and soil conditioners, natural pest controls, pet-care products, and a variety of ways to detoxify chemically abused soil and grow nutrient-rich vegetables. Free catalog. P.O. Box 1447, Fayetteville, AR 72702; (800) 835-0123.

Seeds of Change

Seller of only certified organic, open-pollinated seeds for backyard gardeners. Large selection of heirloom and traditional varieties of vegetable, herb, and flower seeds. Award-winning catalog $3, refundable with your first order. 621 Old Santa Fe Trail, #10, Santa Fe, NM 87501; (505) 983-8956.

Action 76

Cooperative and Community Gardens

Whether you live in the city or country, cooperative gardening is an enjoyable and effective way to provide the hungry with food while building a community and empowering yourself and others. You can start almost anywhere: on the grounds of a church, in a friend's backyard, an abandoned lot, or on land contributed by local officials.

Some cities set aside land for community gardens. Utility companies may make power line rights-of-way available. Senior citizens' centers, youth clubs, and schools may have space for potential garden sites. Some gardens are subdivided into separate plots that are planted, tended, and harvested by individuals and families. Others encourage members to work cooperatively and send produce to needy families, a local soup kitchen, or a food bank. One church terraced the hill behind its building and provided more than one thousand pounds of greens a year for a downtown soup kitchen. Another alternative is to sell the food on Saturday mornings and use the proceeds to feed hungry people.*

What You Can Do

Join a community gardening effort already under way in your neighborhood, or put together a group of your own. For details on how to get started, contact the American Community Gardening Association, 325 Walnut St., Philadelphia, PA 19106; (215) 625-8280. The association publishes a quarterly called *Journal of Community Gardening*.

Action 77

Socially Responsible Food

Now you can shop for a better world with an easy-to-use guide that rates over 2,500 brand-name products, including all major brands of packaged food (from breakfast cereals to pasta sauce), as well as cars, computers, appliances, telephone service, clothing, toys, and other consumer products.

How can you tell if the company that owns the Jolly Green Giant has few women and minorities in top posts or if the makers of Jell-O have a consistently poor record for polluting the environment? *Shopping for a Better World*, published by the Council on Economic Priorities, directs readers to products made by companies that give generously to charities, promote equal opportunity employment, support their communities, and work to keep the environment clean, while helping readers avoid foods that put money in the pockets of tobacco purveyors and those who test products on animals. The guide covers 190 companies, which are rated in eight areas of social responsibility.

*Excerpted with permission from "Hunger Action Handbook," *Seeds* magazine, 1987.

What You Can Do

For information on ordering *Shopping for a Better World*, contact the Council on Economic Priorities, 30 Irving Place, New York, NY 10003-2386; telephone: (800) 729-4CEP or (212) 420-1133; fax: (212) 420-0988.

Chapter 23

Eating as a Political Act: Your Diet and a "Diet for a Small Planet"

Action 78
Sixteen Reasons to Eat Less Meat

While one less steak won't put food in the mouth of a hungry child, cattle raised for beef in the U.S. eat more than enough grain and soy beans to adequately feed the sixty million people that starve to death every year.

As Frances Moore Lappé said years ago, "Every decision we make about the food we eat is a vote for the kind of world we want to live in." No choice better exemplifies that truth than the decision to eat or not eat meat. The consumption of meat plays a major role in the balance of global food resources, the future of our environment, Third World economies, and the humane treatment of animals as well as our own health.*

So, here are sixteen great reasons to eat less (or no) meat!

*Facts and statistics for this action come from John Robbins, *Diet for a New America* (Walpole, NH: Stillpoint, 1987) and the EarthSave Foundation, 706 Frederick St., Santa Cruz, CA 95062. Quoted text is excerpted with permission from "How Our Food Choices Affect the World," *East West: The Journal of Natural Health and Living.*

Livestock Eat Better than Many of the World's Poor

According to the Worldwatch Institute, "Feeding the world's current population on an American diet of 220 grams of grain-fed meat a day would require 2.5 times as much grain as the world's farmers produce for all purposes."

Reason 1. Number of human beings who could be fed annually by grain and soybeans eaten by U.S. livestock: *1.3 billion.*

Reason 2. Number of people who could be adequately fed by the grain saved if Americans reduced their intake of meat by 10 percent: *60 million.*

Reason 3. Pounds of grain and soybeans needed to produce one pound of feedlot beef: *16.*

Reason 4. Percentage of carbohydrates and protein wasted by cycling grain through livestock: *99 and 90.*

Reason 5. Percentage of dietary fiber wasted by cycling grain through livestock: *100.*

Animal Rights

Eating meat, of course, involves killing animals. A single visit to a slaughterhouse has been enough to convert many a meat eater to vegetarianism. One person described the stench of a stockyard as "the smell of bad karma."

Reason 6. Why veal is so tender: *Calves are never allowed to take a single step.*

Reason 7. Why veal is a whitish pink: *Calves are force-fed an anemia-producing diet.*

Reason 8. Number of animals killed for meat per hour in the United States: *500,000.*

Reason 9. Occupation with highest employee turnover rate in the United States: *slaughterhouse worker.*

Reason 10. Occupation with highest employee rate of injury in the United States: *slaughterhouse worker.*

Reason 11. Cost to render an animal unconscious prior to

slaughter so that process is done humanely: *one cent.* Reason given by meat industry for not utilizing this method: *too expensive.*

Even if we have no qualms about the slaughter of animals for food, there are serious environmental and other ethical issues involved. The grazing of cattle, sheep, and goats for meat can have a valid place in an ecologically balanced food economy since not all land is fit for the cultivation of food crops like grains and beans. But the number of animals raised exclusively on rangelands in America is small. Most spend a good part of their lives in feedlots. These are enclosed areas where thousands of animals are crowded together and fattened with a diet of corn, soybeans, and other foods that could be fed to humans. These feedlots amount to animal concentration camps. *Life in the feedlots is so unhealthy that the animals are constantly dosed with antibiotics, which pose health risks for humans.*

Wasted Water

Not only are vast amounts of water polluted by livestock, but even larger amounts are consumed in the breeding process.

Reason 12. Amount of water that goes into the feeding and care of the average cow: *enough to float a destroyer.*

Reason 13. Water needed to produce a pound of wheat: *25 gallons.* Water needed to produce a pound of meat: *2,500 gallons.*

Protecting Our Own Lives

Lastly, we all have our own health, and that of our friends and family, to consider.

Reason 14. Most common cause of death in the United States: *heart attack.* Risk of death from heart attack by average American man consuming a vegetarian diet: *4 percent.*

Reason 15. Increased risk of breast cancer for women who

181

eat meat daily compared to women who eat meat less than once a week: *four times higher.*

Reason 16. Leading source of pesticide residues in the U.S. diet: meat, *55 percent.* Total pesticide residues in U.S. diet supplied by vegetables: *6 percent.* Total pesticide residues in U.S. diet supplied by fruits: *4 percent.* Total pesticide residues in U.S. diet supplied by grains: *1 percent.*

What You Can Do

1. Stop eating meat or reduce your consumption. If and when you do eat meat, select organically fed, humanely treated, free-range beef, lamb, or poultry. Coleman's beef, which is widely distributed, is free of steroids, hormones, and antibodies. It is also very lean, so it has a lower fat content than most of the other beef you will find.
2. Another consideration, if you do choose to eat meat, is the amount of grain it takes to produce each pound of food. According to the USDA, beef requires 16 pounds of grain and soy; pork requires 6 pounds; turkey requires 4 pounds; and broiler chickens require 3 pounds.
3. The following are great resources for more information about adopting a vegetarian diet:

Beyond Beef, by Jeremy Rifkin, is a brilliant examination and indictment of the cattle culture that has come to shape our world.

The Power of Your Plate, by Neil Barnard, is an in-depth discussion of why a high-fiber, low-fat vegetarian diet is optimal for good health.

The Vegetarian Resource Group
P.O. Box 1463
Baltimore, MD 21203
(410) 366-VEGE
This is a nonprofit organization whose goal is to educate the public

about the various aspects of vegetarianism. *The group publishes the*
Vegetarian Journal, *a bimonthly, 36-page publication, as well as*
books, brochures, and posters.

Vegetarian Awareness Network (VEGANET)
P.O. Box 321
Knoxville, TN 37901
(800) USA-VEGE
VEGANET is an all-volunteer, nonsectarian, nonprofit, educational,
social service organization. It networks nationally to advance public
awareness of vegetarianism and can connect you with a local group.

4. Check the shelves of your local library and bookstores for
great vegetarian cookbooks. If you aren't satisfied with the
selection, pick up a copy of the magazine *Vegetarian Times,*
which has a fantastic, satisfaction-guaranteed "Bookshelf"
column in every issue.

Action 79

Eat Fewer Dairy Products

Unfortunately dairy products don't come from happy farm
animals who would rather produce milk, eggs and cheese
than be sent to the slaughterhouse; and their potential negative effect on our health is alarming.

We would like to think we are doing livestock a good
turn by not eating meat, and by substituting cheese,
yogurt, and milk in our diet. But to the compassionate
observer, many dairy farms have little to recommend them
over the feedlot and the slaughterhouse.

In an earlier, more innocent age, milk cows led a quiet,
bucolic life. Ole Bessie roamed hillside pastures and twice
a day was hand-milked in the barn by her owner. She performed a useful service by changing seeds and forage into
food.

Today, this is largely a thing of the past. Very likely, Ole
Bessie is chained for a good part of her life in an enormous

barn with several hundred other cows. She can do little more than eat, lactate, and defecate. This makes her prone to infection, so she receives antibiotics. At milking time, vacuum hoses are attached to her teats as her udders are pumped dry. Like her brothers and sisters in the feedlot, Bessie is treated as little more than a biological machine. As soon as her milk production falls below a certain level, she is sent to the slaughterhouse. Chickens do not fare any better. The typical chicken spends her life in a windowless "factory inside a cage that is one foot high and one foot long." *

Asked what single change in the American diet would produce the greatest health benefit, Washington, D.C. based pediatrician Russell Bunai, says, "Eliminating dairy products." Bunai has observed the effects of cow's milk on the health of children and their families for more than two decades. In the 1960's when he served as a missionary in Ghana, West Africa, Bunai noticed that certain diseases prevalent in areas where people ate dairy were absent in areas free of dairy consumption.

Bunai is not alone in believing that our health would be improved if we cut out dairy. Increasing number of researchers, physicians, nutritionists, and other healthy professionals have found numerous reasons to be wary of dairy, including the following:

✔ Ovarian cancer rates parallel dairy-eating patterns around the world.
✔ Pesticides concentrate in milk of both farm animals and humans.
✔ Antibiotics given to cows can result in drug-resistant bacterial infections in humans, including staph, pneumonia, strep, and tuberculosis.

*Excerpted with permission from *East West: The Journal of Natural Health and Living*.

✔ Although the long-term effects on humans are unknown, the General Accounting Office says that the bovine growth hormone BST [bovine somatotropin, also known as rBGH] increases the risk of mastitis, an udder disease that must be treated with antibiotics.

✔ Cow's milk contains many proteins that are poorly digested and harmful to the human immune system.

✔ Removing dairy from the diet has been shown to shrink enlarged tonsils as well as reduce colds, flus, sinusitis, and ear infections.

✔ Dairy consumption has also been linked to asthma, arthritis, and insulin-dependent diabetes.*

What You Can Do

1. Reduce or eliminate your intake of dairy products. There are some good cookbooks on the market that cater to vegans (vegetarians who do not eat dairy products or animal foods). To learn more about a dairy-free diet, contact:

Vegetarian Awareness Network (VEGANET)
P.O. Box 321
Knoxville, TN 37901
(800) USA-VEGE

The Vegetarian Resource Group
P.O. Box 1463
Baltimore, MD 21203
(410) 366-VEGE

2. When you do buy eggs and dairy products, look for eggs from organically fed, free-range chickens and milk from organically fed cows that aren't treated with BST, and

*Excerpted with permission from "Don't Drink Your Milk," *Natural Health* July/Aug. 1994. For a free trial copy of *Natural Health* magazine, call (800) 925-3330.

shop in health foods stores, food co-ops, and farmers' markets. These are the best places to find dairy products from small farms, which are more likely to treat animals humanely. To find out where you can find BST-free dairy products in your area, contact one of the following organizations:

Mothers and Others for a Livable Planet offers a free "Mothers Milk List" when you join. Phone (212) 242-0010.

National Family Farm Coalition (NEFC) can provide you with a list of producers and stores that are supporting the boycott of BST. Contact the coalition at 110 Maryland Ave., Box 9, Washington, DC 20002; (202) 543-5675.

Action 80

Protect Biodiversity: Eat Brown Eggs

Protect the diversity of species and fight reduction of the gene pool at breakfast!

One hundred species disappear from the planet every day of every year. This reduction in the number of species shrinks the world's genetic pool. Since diversity is a requisite of survival this is a sad and dangerous trend.

One example of this problem is that while there are hundreds of species of chickens, 96 percent of people in the United States eat eggs from only one kind. If that particular strain of bird were attacked by a disease to which it had no resistance, we would be out of eggs overnight. And since all egg-laying chickens are raised by just nine large chicken producers, the chances of such a catastrophe are real: All our eggs are literally in one (genetic) basket.

If you're a passionate or even occasional egg lover there's no reason to quit your job and launch a twenty-four-hour-a-day vigil outside the nearest chicken farm. The problem of a declining egg gene pool can be addressed simply by buying brown eggs. Inside their shells, white and brown eggs are the same—the only difference is in the packaging. If a fair number of people were to make just one small adjustment in their lives and buy brown eggs, they could drastically alter the gene pool. Since the White Leghorn hens that produce most of our eggs cannot lay anything but white eggs, buying brown eggs will create a new market that justifies farmers raising another breed to produce brown eggs. Then at least we would have two major breeds of chickens producing eggs in this country instead of one. It wouldn't make a huge change in the gene pool or in the world, but wouldn't you rather sail on a ship with two lifeboats instead of one?*

What You Can Do

1. Eat brown eggs—preferably from free-range, organically fed chickens.
2. Eggs are not the only food that deserve our consideration before we buy. Another example is salmon, most of which are ocean-farmed. These ocean-farmed populations are soaring, and in the process they're changing the natural balance in their water ecosystems because they are out-competing other species. Farmed freshwater fish, like trout, are a better choice, because they do not compete.
3. To learn more about the ecology of food, read *Seeds of Change,* by Kenny Ausubel (San Francisco: HarperCollins, 1994.

Action 81

Tales of Coffee, Coconuts, Cashews, and Cocoa

Imported food items are often to blame for the poverty and destruction of local agriculture in much of Central and South America.

Considering the current level of regular and massive consumption of such items as sugar, coffee, cocoa, tea, and tropical

*Excerpted with permission from Marty Teitel, "Activism in Everyday Life," *Utne Reader,* March/April 1988.

fruits, it's hard to believe these products were foreign to American diets barely one hundred years ago. Once we acquired a taste for these luxuries, nothing stopped us in our pursuit of them, including the near-total destruction of local agricultural practices in much of Central and South America.

In some regions plantations were immediately established to raise these products on a massive scale. In others, taxation forced small farmers to cultivate export cash crops, and eventually, in hard times, they were forced to sell off their land to large owners. In most areas the net result was the same. The agricultural land was concentrated in the hands of a few national or foreign concerns, and most of it was used for the cultivation of export cash crops. Land used for domestic food production decreased. Many peasants who were once self-sufficient farmers ended up deprived of even a garden plot and became dependent for survival on imported foods, which could be acquired with cash earned by employment on the plantations. Our powerful agricultural interests bound these peasants to a life of poverty and hunger.

Although most of these countries are now independent, little has changed. In the "banana republics" of Central America, in the coffee-growing nations of sub-Saharan Africa, in the sugar producing areas of the Philippines, the agricultural, social and economic situation is essentially the same. Most of the land is used for cash crops and is controlled by a native elite or by multinational corporations.

The problems of social and economic justice, poverty, hunger and famine in the Third World are complex ones. But, at least, we should be aware that our choices in the supermarket are intimately related to them.*

---

*Reprinted with permission from *East West: The Journal of Natural Health and Living*. All rights reserved.

What You Can Do

Purchase tropically grown foods from small businesses and worker-owned cooperatives in Third World countries. Many products are available, from coffee and sugar to tea, vanilla, sesame tahini, and nuts. Fruit is usually not handled by these organizations, and it is best to purchase locally grown, in-season products. Ask at your local natural foods stores or consult the resources below.

1. Coffee grown in Central America tends to enter this country in its raw form. These beans are then roasted and put on the market. This may seem logical to you, but what it means is that the farmers make about $60 per 100-pound bag, while the roasters make an average of $400 per 100-pound bag. Cafe Britt is a Costa Rican company that roasts its own beans and returns the bulk of the profits to the farmers. Its coffee is exceptional and relatively inexpensive. To order, call (800) GO BRITT.

2. Cultural Survival Enterprises, the nonprofit marketing division of Cultural Survival, Inc. (a nonprofit human rights organizations), imports sustainably harvested, non-timber forest products, such as nuts, oils, honey, and beeswax, the sale of which furthers efforts to protect endangered ecosystems and support communities around the world. For more information and a catalog of its products, contact it at this address:

Cultural Survival, Inc.
46 Brattle St.
Cambridge, MA 02138
(617) 621-3818

Chapter 24

Helping the Hungry

The Greater Chicago Food Depository looks no different from the warehouses that surround it in an otherwise residential neighborhood on Chicago's West Side. What distinguishes it are the row of volunteers at work on a unique production line and the product that is stacked around them—food, tons of food. Huge shipments of cereal, market over-orders, misprinted labels, discontinued products, dented cans, crushed boxes. The depository is the last refuge of forgotten foods.

In 1992 the Greater Chicago Food Depository distributed over 22 million pounds of food: 48,000 meals for every operating day, $45 million worth of food. Those numbers make it the largest food bank in the world. The food depository is feeding a hungry city. Other food banks like it are feeding a hungry country. Almost 30 years after the United States initiated its war on hunger with various forms of federal assistance, the specter of chronic hunger is once again threatening the country's most vulnerable citizens.

In March 1993, the United States reached a distressing milestone: A record 27.4 million people—about 10 percent of the nation's population and 9 million more than as recently as 1989—were receiving food stamps. Between half a million and a million of the country's senior citizens regularly skip meals. Native American reservations, where people have trouble reaching U.S. government support services, remain often startling pockets of hunger. The hungry can be found among the nation's homeless and undocumented immigrants. But mostly, the hungry in the United States are still children. One child in four grows up hungry, according to Bread for the World, a Washington-based international, interfaith policy agency.

While the grim numbers indicate a serious problem, hunger experts note that people in the United States are not facing the dire starvation situations experienced by people in other parts of the world. "We don't have people starving to death in the streets," says John Colgan, director of the Illinois Hunger Coalition, "but we do have over 30 million people who do not have the food security they need to maintain an adequate diet."*

Action 82

Feeding the Hungry in Your Community

Hunger is being fought on many fronts—from short-term solutions, helping provide a hot meal to someone who doesn't know where their next meal is coming from, to medium-term solutions, organizing to open a soup kitchen or doing food stamp outreach, to long-term solutions, supporting legislation, creating jobs and building low-income housing. Though it might sound a bit overwhelming at first, the following list describes some simple actions that make it easy to get started. Once you find an action that appeals to you, the next step is to hook up with a local hunger group that needs your help."†

*Excerpted with permission from "Who's Hungry Now," by Kevin Clarke, which appeared in the Christian social justice magazine *Salt*, March 1993. (Subscription information from 205 W. Monroe St., Chicago, IL 60606.)
†Excerpted with permission from the "Hunger Action Handbook," *Seeds* magazine, 1987.

What You Can Do

1. Volunteer to cook and serve food in a soup kitchen two to three hours a week.
2. Volunteer to pick up donated food.
3. Offer the use of your car or van to assist those working in a soup kitchen with food deliveries.
4. Donate kitchen equipment. Coffeemakers, cutting boards, pots and pans, and utensils are often welcome.
5. Donate food (see Action 83, Food Banks).
6. Offer to help out in an office answering phones, writing letters, or raising funds.
7. If you have special skills, such as in public relations, computer operations, grant writing, or warehouse management, you might be able to provide a group with technical assistance.
8. If you're in printing, restaurant management, advertising, or transportation, your business can probably help you play an important role, too.

Taking the Next Step: Now you're ready to pick up the phone and get a list of the local hunger groups in your area. Start by calling your church or synagogue, the mayor's office, or check the Yellow Pages under "Social Service Agencies."

Let the group know that you want to help and tell them a bit about what you might like to do, or feel free to ask them for suggestions. Let them know the amount of time you're willing to invest and what, if any, resources you're willing to contribute.*

If you don't have any luck, there are many national organizations that will be happy to help you locate a local group. Some of them include:

---

*The text of this section is excerpted with permission from the "Hunger Action Handbook," *Seeds* magazine, 1987.

Results
236 Massachusetts Ave., NE
Suite 300
Washington, DC 20002
(202) 543-9340
Results is a nonprofit, grassroots organization dedicated to creating the political will to end hunger. There are local Results groups active in more than 100 communities nationwide.

World Hunger Year (WHY)
505 8th Ave., 21st Floor
New York, NY 10018
(212) 629-8850
WHY is a nonprofit organization that works to inform the general public, the media, and policy makers about the extent and causes of hunger in the United States and abroad.

For more hunger resources, see Action 88.

Action 83

Food Banks: A Second Harvest for the Hungry

When the Parker Meridien Hotel in New York City offered Helen Palit a two-ton chocolate Statue of Liberty left over from the bicentennial celebration, Ms. Palit knew exactly what to do.

She telephoned one of her co-workers to "come at midnight with a crowbar." Within hours, the chocolate was broken up and delivered to a drug-rehabilitation program for patients in the New York region who required large doses of sugar as part of their treatment.

Ms. Palit is the founder and executive director of City Harvest, a nonprofit food bank that collects excess food and distributes it to soup kitchens, drug-rehabilitation centers, homeless shelters, and other programs for the hungry in New York.

While donations of giant chocolate statues are rare, for the first six years the agency's vans have picked up and distributed more than 5,000 pounds a day of New York City's choices leftovers to the hungry.

Much of the leftover food comes from upscale restaurants and their suppliers. But there are other sources as well: 50,000 bottles of orange juice from a failed orange juice enterprise; 500 live chickens, left over from a commercial photography shoot; and 100 boxed lunches from a brokerage firm luncheon that was canceled.

"The United States Department of Agriculture estimates that twenty percent of all food produced in the United States is wasted," Ms. Palit said. "There is enough food in this city to feed every hungry person; it is just a matter of logistics."*

What You Can Do

Your local food bank needs your help. To locate the food bank nearest you, consult your local yellow pages or contact Second Harvest, 116 South Michigan Ave., Suite 4, Chicago, IL 60603; (312) 263-2303. Consider volunteering in a food warehouse, sorting contributed food, assisting with pickups or deliveries, and, of course, donating food.

Action 84

Be a Voice for Hungry Children

Hunger is very much a children's issue. One in four children is hungry and the ranks of hungry kids continue to grow. The problem is not a lack of funds but a poor use of the funds we currently spend to assist children in need.

The sad fact is that for every dollar that goes to feed an expectant mother or a hungry child, the government can save four dollars in health care costs for low-birth-weight infants and malnourished children. Hunger is causing children to do poorly

*Reprinted by permission from the New York Times Company.

in school and weakening America's future workforce. From a purely human point of view, no child should ever go hungry. Add to that the cold, hard economic costs of hunger, and there is absolutely no excuse.

What You Can Do

Hungry children don't have a voice in Congress, yet every year important pieces of legislation come up that directly affect them. Head Start, child support enforcement, school lunches, and many other issues are affected by legislation at the national level.

Children need advocates who are willing to follow legislation that affects them and who will lobby on their behalf. Small actions, like phone calls and postcards to members of Congress, can produce impressive results on crucial votes.

Ben & Jerry's, the ice cream people, and the Children's Defense Fund have created the Call for Kids Campaign to keep you informed about child-related legislation. Before important votes, it will advise you on whom to contact to make your voice heard.

Call for Kids Campaign
c/o Ben & Jerry's
Box 240
Waterbury, VT 05676
(800) 255-4371

Children's Defense Fund
25 E St., NW
Washington, DC 20001
(202) 628-8787

Action 85
Freedom from Hunger

It is one thing to provide food to hungry people during an emergency; it is another to solve the deeper problem of chronic hunger and malnutrition among the poor rural populations of the world. The philosophy of Freedom from Hunger's self-help program "Credit with Education" is effectively rendered by the proverb "Feed a man a fish and he'll eat for a day; teach him to fish and he'll eat for a lifetime." Over one billion people—one-sixth of the world's population—suffer from hunger and malnutrition, and long-term, sustainable solutions are needed if we are to ensure the basic human right of freedom from hunger for all people.

Credit with Education provides communities in Africa, Asia, and Latin America with resources and information, both of which are sorely needed. The program provides monetary credit, in the form of small loans amounting to about $60, that people can put to use in an income-generating activity they already know how to do, such as making clothes or raising chickens; the education component promotes good breast-feeding, weaning, diarrhea prevention and management techniques, and family planning practices.

Women are the primary focus of the Credit with Education program because of the central role they play as caretakers of and providers for their families. Women and girls bear the greatest burden of poverty and are frequently more malnourished than men and boys. This exacerbates the cycle of hunger because their children become hunger's most vulnerable victims.

For nearly fifty years, Freedom from Hunger has been developing programs to reduce chronic hunger. As an American organization, Freedom from Hunger also feels a special obligation to the estimated twenty-five million chronically hungry people in the United States. They are looking at the feasibility of introducing a modified version of Credit with Education in the United States. Currently Freedom from Hunger has community health advisers working in the American South, where they follow a strategy originally developed overseas.

What You Can Do

The multi-country continuation and expansion of Credit with Education will continue into 1998. You can help by sending tax-deductible donations to Freedom from Hunger at 1644 DaVinci Court, Davis, CA 95616. To give you an idea of what a financial contribution can accomplish, Freedom from Hunger offers this breakdown:

- ✔ $20 a year would enable one woman to join a Freedom from Hunger credit association.
- ✔ $100 per year would allow five women to join.
- ✔ $600 per year over a five-year period would maintain a whole credit association of women (20–30 women).
- ✔ $1,200 per year over a five-year period would maintain two credit associations.
- ✔ $3,000 per year over a five-year period would allow for the start-up of five new credit associations.

Please keep in mind that these are only guidelines. Freedom from Hunger accepts gifts of all sizes and wants people to know that any amount helps.

Supporting Freedom from Hunger's Credit with Education program is a real opportunity to make a difference in the lives of a great many hard-pressed women and families worldwide.

Action 86

Bread for the World: Passing Legislation to End World Hunger

Bread for the World is an organization that does *not* provide direct relief or development assistance. Rather, it works to persuade Congress and the president's administration to implement policies that deal with the root causes of hunger and poverty.

How does it do this? Each year, the group conducts a letter-writing campaign in which thousands of letters are sent to senators and representatives about a specific piece of legislation. Over fifty thousand individuals across the country respond to "action alerts" advising them on legislation before Congress. Additional suggestions on other effective actions are included.

In addition to a letter-writing campaign, a Quickline network enables all members to flood congressional offices with telephone calls in rapid response to critical events in the legislative process. Background papers and other educational materials provide vital information to support these campaigns.

This national movement of citizen advocates has achieved impressive results. Among its accomplishments:

- ✔ In 1986, Bread for the World members were instrumental in getting tax-reform legislation passed so that six million of America's lowest-income working families and individuals were relieved of the burden of unjust taxes.
- ✔ In 1987, Bread for the World played a key role in helping to pass legislation for a $73 million increase in funding for the women, infants, and children's food and nutrition program.
- ✔ In 1990, debt relief provisions promoted by Bread for the World were included in the 1990 farm bill, reducing food aid–related debts of poor countries and freeing money for investment in health care, education, and other needs.
- ✔ In 1992, thanks to Bread for the World leadership, the Horn of Africa Recovery and Food Security Act became law, redirecting U.S. government priorities from Cold War purposes to support for peace, democracy, and grassroots development.
- ✔ In 1993, Bread for the World's "Every Fifth Child Act" helped win almost $2 billion in increases for WIC (the women, infants, and children supplemental food program), Head Start, and the Job Corps.
- ✔ Bread for the World has been awarded the Presidential End Hunger Award (1990) and the International Child Survival Award (1994), and its annual hunger report was honored as the "Best Hunger Resource" (1992).

What You Can Do

Join Bread for the World in its fight to pass legislation to make effective federal and international programs aimed at alleviating hunger and poverty and to gain additional understanding about the true causes of hunger. Contact the group at 1100 Wayne Ave., Suite 1000, Silver Spring, MD 20910; (301) 608-2400.

Bread for the World also has an excellent catalog of books and information on how to organize in your own community, plus easy tips on how to write effective letters, communicate with media representatives, and speak with your local elected officials. Request the catalog when you contact the organization.

Action 87
Food First

Food First, also known as the Institute for Food and Development Policy, is a nonprofit research and education center dedicated to investigating and exposing the root causes of hunger. It was founded in 1975 by Frances Moore Lappé, author of the best-selling *Diet for a Small Planet,* and Dr. Joseph Collins. Food First research has documented how hunger is created by concentrated economic and political power, not by scarcity. Resources and decision making in the hands of a wealthy few deprive the majority of land, jobs, and therefore food.

Hailed by the *New York Times* as "one of the most established food think tanks in the country," the institute has profoundly shaped the debate about hunger and Third World development. The institute is, however, more than a think tank. Through books, reports, school curricula, audiovisual materials, media appearances, and speaking engagements, Food First experts not only reveal the often hidden roots of hunger but also show individuals how to get involved in bringing an end to the problem. Food First inspires action by highlighting the courageous efforts of people around the world who are creating farming and food systems that effectively feed the poor. As a member of Food First you can join a worldwide network of people working for a world free of hunger and injustice.

Two books of note—*Diet for a Small Planet* by Frances Moore Lappé and *Food First: Beyond the Myth of Scarcity*—have provided the background and conceptual framework for much of the best research being done today on hunger issues. These books are essential reading for anyone who wants a deeper understanding of the problem.

Other publications include:

Betraying the National Interest: How U.S. Foreign Aid Threatens Global Security by Undermining the Economic Stability of the Third World, by Frances Moore Lappé, Rachel Schuman, and Kevin Danaher (Oakland, CA: Food First Books).

World Hunger: Twelve Myths, upon which the introduction to this section of the book is based, by Frances Moore Lappé (New York: Joseph Collins/Food First Books).

Action Alerts on Brazil, Central America, Honduras, Nicaragua, South Africa, foreign aid, the debt crisis, and family farms are available for fifty cents each.

Food First provides a constant flow of information and ideas about action to ensure that you can play an effective role in the struggle to end hunger and fight injustice in the Third World.

What You Can Do

Become a member of Food First today. Send $30 ($20 if you consider yourself low-income) to 398 60th St., Oakland, CA 94618; telephone (510) 654-4400; fax (510) 654-4551; E-mail: foodfirst@igc.apc.org.

Action 88

Other Organizations Working to Fight Hunger

The following is a select list of only a small number of the many organizations working to fight hunger.

Food Research and Action Center
1875 Connecticut Ave., NW

Suite 540
Washington, DC 20009
(202) 986-2200
This nonprofit, nonpartisan center works with individuals, elected offi-
cials, religious groups, and civic leaders to improve federal food pro-
grams, to seek greater opportunities for low-income people, and to protect
the rights of the poor.

Interfaith Hunger Appeal
475 Riverside Dr.
Suite 1630
New York, NY 10115-0079
(212) 870-2035
This hunger-awareness project, sponsored by the American Jewish Joint
Distribution Committee, Catholic Relief Services, Church World
Service, and Lutheran World Relief, conducts hunger and development
programs in over one hundred countries, including the United States.

National Student Campaign against Hunger and
Homelessness
29 Temple Place
Boston, MA 02111
(617) 292-4823
This is the largest network of student hunger activists in the United
States. Launched by the Public Interest Research Groups (PIRGs) in
cooperation with USA for Africa, it works with colleges and high
schools to sponsor programs that offer immediate relief to the hungry and
homeless, as well as longer-term projects that address the causes of
hunger.

Oxfam America
26 West St.
Boston, MA 02111
(617) 482-1211
Oxfam is an international nonprofit agency that, in partnership with
poor people around the world, works to end hunger. Oxfam funds local
groups working to increase their food production and economic self-

reliance. These projects are designed, implemented, and run by people in the local communities.

World Hunger Year
505 8th Ave., 21st Floor
New York, NY 10018
Telephone: (212) 629-8850
Fax: (212) 465-9274
Dedicated to the reality that "every year is world hunger year until hunger is ended."

Part VI

Socially Responsible Banking and Investing

 Putting your money to work on the world's problems

Chapter 25

"It's 9:00 P.M.: Do You Know Where Your Money Is?"

Money carries the values of the person whose pocket it happens to be sitting in—for as long as it sits there. When a dollar passes out of your hand to purchase a product, acquire a service, make an investment, contribute to a worthy cause, or even be parked briefly in your checking account—you are casting a vote. It is a vote cast for a particular company or institution, the quality of its product or service, its management, the way it treats its employees, whether or not it chooses to protect the environment, accept government defense contracts, or purchase supplies from minority businesses.

There is a direct and tangible connection between every investment or financial transaction you make and the values that are promoted throughout the world. While we may not all own stocks and bonds, most of us have checking accounts, some types of insurance, and perhaps IRAs. When you pay your premiums, deposit your paycheck, or purchase something with a credit card, you are selecting a temporary custodian of your money. The moment a dollar leaves your hand, it can be used to make the world a more dangerous place for generations to come, or it can be invested in your dreams and hopes for the world your children will grow up in.

The chapter title is a headline from a Working Assets advertisement.

Chapter 26

Socially Responsible Banking, Financing Affordable Housing, and Supporting Small Business

Action 89
Is Your Local Bank Helping or Hurting Your Community?

Let's examine this more closely, taking as an example your local bank. If you deposit your paycheck on a Friday, by Tuesday or Wednesday you might have access to those funds. While the screen on the automated teller machine confirms that the money is in your account, and you might think that your hard-earned dollars are sitting safely in the bank's vault—this is far from the real story. Before the money is even available to you, your bank has collected the funds and put your paycheck to work. It may have loaned your money out to a local McDonald's franchise or to a real estate developer or financed the military purchases of a repressive government—all without

Sources for this section include: Co-op America's *Socially Responsible Financial Planning Handbook*. For information on ordering a copy, see Action 94.

your knowledge or consent. While it's true that federal regulations and the bank's own need for cash might cause 15 percent of your paycheck to be kept on hand, the other 85 percent is usually hard at work within one day of your deposit.

If you don't know where your money is, what it's financing, or whom it's being loaned to, there's a very good chance some of it is being used to destroy the environment or build weapons or is being put to some other use that would offend your values and ethics. But the moment it leaves your hands, you've effectively surrendered control and given up responsibility for it.

Don't choose a bank blindly. Under the Community Reinvestment Act of 1977, each bank and thrift (savings and loans) must issue a statement that identifies its community's needs and discusses ways in which it is helping meet those needs through programs, services, and lending practices. Institutions are given a rating by federal regulators. This rating is public information. Also of public interest is written correspondence concerning community involvement, which each institution is required to keep on file.

What You Can Do

1. Call the main offices of your bank and other local banks to request their Community Reinvestment Act Statements and their Community Reinvestment Act Performance Evaluations. You may also want to look at the public comment file for each institution. Not only will you get useful information, but the mere act of contacting the banks will send the message that people really are monitoring their community involvement.

2. If you are not satisfied with banks in your local area or would prefer to invest in banks whose values are closer to your own, consider one of the institutions listed in the next two actions, or contact one of the following resources:

The Adams National Bank
1627 K St., NW
Washington, DC 20036

(202) 466-4090
A women-owned bank. Contact for information about banking services.

Black Enterprise
Attn.: Circulation
130 Fifth Ave.
New York, NY 10111
(212) 242-8000
Send $6.95 for its annual publication of the top 100 African-American–owned businesses, which includes banks, savings and loans, and insurance companies (a new listing is issued each June).

Cannicor
P.O. Box 426829
San Francisco, CA 94142
(415) 885-5102.
Cannicor is an interfaith council on corporate accountability that rates banks for social responsibility. Contact it for information on socially responsible banks.

National Bankers Association
1802 T St., NW
Washington, DC 20009
(202) 588-5432
It can provide you with a list of minority-owned banks.

The Women's National Bank
821 17th St.
Denver, CO 80202
(303) 293-2265
Contact this women-owned bank for information about banking services.

Action 90

Banking on Low-Income Communities

There was a time when local banks had a vested interest in investing in their communities. After all, they were members of the communities, and what was good for main street was good for banks. For most banks this is no longer the case. Once mortgages and other longer-term loans are made, local banks sell them to other institutions. The new holders of these loans, which are usually located out of state, have no interest in building communities. They're looking for safe bets that will make them money. The result is that it can be very difficult for low-income communities to get loans.

Take the South Shore area of Chicago, for example. It used to be characterized by high unemployment, abandoned and deteriorating housing, failing small businesses—and not one bank willing to make an investment in the community to try to turn the situation around. All that changed in 1975, when a group of social entrepreneurs purchased the local bank and began to alter the face of community development banking. Within a short time the newly formed South Shore Bank was pumping money into the South Shore area. Housing was renovated; hundreds of small businesses found financing; students borrowed money for education; more money was loaned to local nonprofit agencies to assure that needed human services would be provided to local residents. Jobs were created, the area's physical appearance improved, and foundations were laid for a healthier future.

The South Shore Bank accomplished a feat no other bank ever had before: the revitalization of a neighborhood that everyone thought was beyond hope. It also proved that community development banking makes good business sense. Today the bank is fiscally sound and continues to invest in depressed Chicago neighborhoods.

South Shore Bank's success has inspired other small banks in communities across the country. Wherever you live, you can enjoy the service of any of these caring, well-run commercial banks that put your money to work building low-income housing, financing small minority-owned businesses in some of America's most economically depressed neighborhoods, or supporting other community economic development activities. Your deposits earn competitive interest income and are insured by the FDIC up to $100,000.

What You Can Do

Contact any of the banks listed below to ask for an application, current interest rates, a list of all banking services, and information about community investment activities.

Blackfeet National Bank
P.O. Box 730
Browning, MT 59417-0730
(406) 338-7000
$100 minimum deposit to open a checking account
$25 minimum deposit to open a savings account

Community Capital Bank
111 Livingston St.
Brooklyn, NY 11201-9215
(800) 827-6699 or (718) 802-1212
$1,000 minimum deposit to open a checking account
No minimum deposit to open a savings account

Elk Horn Bank & Trust
P.O. Box 248
Arkadelphia, AR 71923
(501) 246-5811
$1,500 minimum deposit to open a Super Now checking account
$100 minimum deposit to open a savings account.

NCB Savings Bank
139 S. High St.
Hillsboro, OH 45133
(800) 322-1251or (513) 393-4246
$100 minimum deposit to open a checking account
$100 minimum deposit to open a savings account

South Shore Bank
71st & Jeffery Blvd.
Chicago, IL 60649

(800) NOW-SSBK or (312) 753-5636
$100 minimum deposit to open a checking account
$250 minimum deposit to open a savings account

Vermont National Bank
Socially Responsible Banking Fund
P.O. Box 804
Brattleboro, VT 05302
(800) 772-3863 or (802) 257-7151
No minimum deposit to open either a checking or a savings
account

Action 91

Community Development Credit Unions

Community development credit unions (CDCUs) are financial
service cooperatives that are democratically controlled by residents of the low-income communities they serve. They have no
other agenda than to support their low-income members.

Unlike traditional banks, credit unions are owned entirely by
their depositors; they are financial cooperatives. In the case of
community development credit unions, the depositors are mostly low-income and oftentimes minorities. CDCUs recycle their
members' insured savings for loans that promote neighborhood
revitalization and growth. They provide financing for housing
rehabilitation and acquisition, small and minority businesses,
cooperatives, and nonprofits, as well as for family and personal
needs. All loans are made to individual members and member
institutions, keeping the assets of the community within the
community. CDCUs confront the Catch-22 of low-income bor-
rowers who can't get loans because they lack credit histories and
can't build credit records because they can't get loans.

Many CDCUs also stem the flow of money that usually runs
out of low-income areas to nonresident owners of land, housing,
retail stores, and large businesses that service these areas.
Members of CDCUs empower one another to take ownership
positions in their own communities.

Most CDCUs offer federally insured deposits up to $100,000

and have not experienced the problems confronting the savings and loan industry. Assets range in size from $100,000 to more than $40 million in the approximately 300 CDCUs nationwide.

The National Federation of Community Development Credit Unions (NFCDCU) is the countrywide membership association of credit unions serving predominantly low-income communities. It is a national clearinghouse for information on CDCUs, operates many programs in support of existing CDCUs, and actively participates in the chartering of community development credit unions. More than one-third of the CDCUs in the United States are members of the national federation.

What You Can Do

To find out about the CDCU nearest you, CDCUs in general, and how you can become involved by opening an account, contact the National Federation of Community Development Credit Unions at 120 Wall St., 10th Floor, New York, NY 10005-3902; (212) 809-1851.

Action 92

Community Development Loan Funds

Poverty, despite popular misconceptions, results not so much from a lack of resources or capabilities as from the patterns of ownership of land, housing, businesses and financial institutions that drain the resources out of lower income communities.
—National Association of Community Development
Loan Funds

Community development loan funds (CDLFs) represent another approach to the same problems that the South Shore Bank of Chicago and community development credit unions seek to address. CDLFs are unique in both structure and mode of operation. They are designed quite specifically as vehicles for socially responsible investors to lend money indirectly to community land trusts, housing cooperatives, community development corporations, worker-owned/cooperative businesses, and other projects involving low-income individuals who would otherwise have no access to credit or capital. A CDLF is committed to building social and economic justice in a specific community by promoting the development of businesses and institutions that strengthen the economic base of that community.

CDLFs are often "lenders of last resort," providing capital when no other financial institution will do so or at least providing funds at rates that are affordable to the recipient. Community development loan funds are an excellent way for you to put your money to work in grassroots community-building. While these funds tend to have low yields, they are also safe investments, and the income is tax-deductible.

Currently the National Association of Community Development Loan Funds (NACDLF) has more than forty member funds you can choose from.

What You Can Do

For more information about community development loan funds and a listing of individual funds, contact the NACDLF, 924 Cherry St., 3d Floor, Philadelphia, PA 19107-2405; (215) 923-4754.

Action 93
Community Land Trusts

A community land trust (CLT) is a nonprofit corporation created to acquire and hold land for the benefit of a local community. Land trusts ensure the availability of housing for low- and moderate-income residents and also provide general access to and preservation of undeveloped land.

Take a low-income family living in the worst substandard housing, and add up how much rent it will pay over its lifetime. Even at today's prices, unadjusted for inflation, over forty years it would pay ten to fifteen times the current market value of the housing it occupies. A middle- or upper-income person

213

with a bank mortgage will pay only three or four times the market value of the home he or she owns (as a result of mortgage interest). CLTs try to provide poor people with an alternative. There are currently more than seventy-five CLTs around the nation, mostly in New England.

Once formed, a typical CLT will purchase run-down homes in neighborhoods that appear destined for gentrification, commercialization, or other kinds of development. Volunteer work by CLT members brings the dwellings up to habitable standards. Each dwelling will then be sold to a low-income applicant, but the deed to the land will be held by the trust. Often, the CLT will rent the home for a few months to the buyer, with the accumulated rental fees put toward a down payment. Unlike traditional buyers moving into the neighborhood, the CLT homeowner benefits little if prices begin to soar.

"The theory is that the owner gets back whatever he puts in, plus an adjustment for inflation during the period, but does not receive the added value that the community has given the home," says Chuck Matthei, director of the Institute for Community Economics. In that way, formerly distressed properties in now-rehabilitated neighborhoods can be kept for low- and middle-income people. Each CLT sets its own formula for maximum allowable income and family size to qualify for a home. Often consideration is given to people who already live in the neighborhood or who have recently been displaced from it.

What You Can Do

Contact the Institute for Community Economics at (413) 746-8660, or write to it at 57 School St., Springfield, MA 01105, for a list of CLTs, news on local and national meetings, technical literature on how to start a CLT, and information on how to make a loan to a CLT or to subscribe to its newsletter, *Community Economics.*

Chapter 27

Socially Responsible Investing

Action 94

Money Markets and Mutual Funds .

Most money market and mutual funds are likely to invest in business and government activities that conflict with your own social concerns and values. Whether it's Dow Chemical's destruction of the ozone, General Electric's nuclear weapons production, or Scott Paper's assault on Indonesian rain forests, most funds own stocks in companies whose policies will offend almost anyone.

In the first edition of this book there were so few socially responsible funds that we could profile each one, but things have changed a great deal since 1990. Investors have poured more than $2.5 billion into socially responsible funds, and you now have over twenty-five funds to choose from. The growth of socially responsible investing allows you to pick funds not only on the basis of performance but also of the criteria they use for selecting which investments they make.

Investment criteria, as well as investment strategy, vary from fund to fund. Most funds rely on what are called "negative

Sources for this section include Co-op America's *Socially Responsible Financial Planning Handbook.*

screens" to make their investments; funds might screen out companies involved in nuclear energy, animal testing, or weapons production. The other screens used are positive ones: investing in companies that conserve natural resources, promote women and minorities, or give large charitable donations. Be aware that some funds, like the Working Assets family of funds, have strict, well-defined social investment criteria while others, like the Dreyfus Third Century Fund, have less rigorous screens. No fund is perfect, so you need to decide what you can live with.

What You Can Do

1. Contact the following investment institutions, and request a prospectus for each of their socially responsible funds. The prospectus will tell you how the fund has performed, where the money is invested, and what screens are applied to the investments. All of these institutions offer both money market funds and mutual funds. (If you'd like more information about these two types of funds, see no. 2 below.)

Calvert Group
4550 Montgomery Ave.
Suite 1000 N
Bethesda, MD 20814
(800) 368-2748

Covenant Portfolio
309 W. Washington St.
Suite 1300
Chicago, IL 60606
(800) 878-7862 or (312) 443-8472

Domini Social Index Trust
Signature Financial Group, Inc.

6 St. James Ave.
Boston, MA 02116
(800) 762-6814

Dreyfus Third Century Fund
EAB Plaza East Tower
Uniondale, NY 11556
(800) 782-6620

Green Century Funds
29 Temple Place
Suite 200
Boston, MA 02111
(800) 934-7336 or (617) 482-0800

New Alternatives Fund
150 Broadhollow Rd.
Melville, NY 11747
(516) 466-0808

Parnassus Fund
244 California St.
San Francisco, CA 94111
(800) 999-3505 or (415) 362-3505

Pax World Fund, Inc.
224 State St.
Portsmouth, NH 03801
(800) 767-1729 or (603) 431-8022

Progressive Environmental Fund
44 Wall Street Equity Group
26 Broadway
Suite 205
New York, NY 10004
(800) 543-2620

Rightime Social Awareness
Lincoln Investment
Forst Pavilion
218 Glenside Ave.
Wyncote, PA 19095
(800) 242-1421 or (215) 242-1421

Working Assets Capital Management
1 Harbour Place
Suite 525
Portsmouth, NH 03801
(800) 533-3862 or (603) 436-5152

The following offer socially responsible money market funds:

Community Capital Bank
111 Livingston St.
Brooklyn, NY 11201-9215
(800) 827-6699 or (718) 802-1212

NCB Savings Bank
139 S. High St.
Hillsboro, OH 45133
(800) 322-1251 or (513) 393-4246

South Shore Bank
71st & Jeffery Blvd.
Chicago, IL 60649
(800) NOW-SSBK or (312) 753-5636

Vermont National Bank
Socially Responsible Banking Fund
P.O. Box 804
Brattleboro, VT 05302
(800) 772-3863 or (802) 257-7151

2. An excellent resource for anyone new to investing or new to socially responsible investing, is Co-op America's *Socially Responsible Financial Planning Handbook.* To order a copy, send $5 to Co-op America, 1850 M Street, NW, Suite 700, Washington, DC 20036; (202) 872-5307.

3. Good Money Publications, Inc., offers *Good Money's Social Funds Guide.* To receive a copy, send $32.95 to Good Money Publications, P.O. Box 363, Worcester, VT 05682; telephone (800) 535-3551; fax (802) 223-8949.

Action 95
Investment Advisers and Newsletters

The socially responsible investment movement has spawned a fairly large group of advisers who specialize in selecting investment opportunities that can meet both social and financial goals. Because each of the companies and individuals has a different fee schedule and widely varying track records, you should carefully investigate before selecting one.

Perhaps the best way to proceed is to join the Social Investment Forum, a national association of professional financial advisers, brokers, managers, bankers, analysts, and investors. The forum publishes guides that will help you begin the selection process, including *Social Investment Services: A Guide to Forum Members,* which lists all of its professional members and the services they provide. The forum also publishes a quarterly newsletter and *Socially Screened Mutual Funds: Performance and Benchmark Comparison Chart,* with periodic updates on socially responsible investment trends.

It's significant that by the end of 1993, $700 billion was invested in the United States with some type of social screen, up from $450 billion in 1988. This includes substantial funds controlled by some of the nation's most respected colleges and universities, pension funds, and insurance companies, as well as many funds controlled by city and state governments.

What You Can Do

1. The Social Investment Forum offers individual and institutional memberships. For information, contact Social Investment Forum, 121 Mt. Vernon St., Boston, MA 02108; telephone: (617) 723-7171; fax: (617) 723-7105. Benefits include seminars, national quarterly meetings, and a quarterly newsletter.

2. Another good resource is the Investor Responsibility Research Center, an independent, nonprofit organization that provides reporting, analysis, and software to institutional investors and others. For more information, contact the center at 1350 Connecticut Ave., NW, Suite 700, Washington, DC 20036; telephone: (202) 833-0700; fax (202) 833-3555.

3. Subscribe to one or more of the newsletters that monitor the socially responsible investment industry, the social performance of American businesses, and strategies for managing your investments in a responsible manner. Some of the most helpful of these publications include:

Clean Yield. This monthly newsletter focuses on publicly traded companies that make, buy, sell, or hold recommendations on the basis of companies' financial performance, future outlook, and socially responsible behavior. It discusses major trends in the marketplace and the impact these trends are expected to have on the stock market. Clean Yield Group also publishes a model portfolio of recommended stocks, which, from March 1985 to December 1993, outperformed the Standard & Poor's 500 stock index by more than 80 percent! Available for $95 from *Clean Yield,* P.O. Box 1880, Greensboro Bend, VT 05842; phone: (802) 533-7178; or fax: (802) 533-2907.

Good Money: The First Newsletter for Socially Concerned Investors. Published bimonthly, it helps investors explore the relationship between corporate ethics, social responsibility, and the selection of investment opportunities with strong financial returns. The focus is on large, publicly traded corporations. *Good Money* also tracks its own list of socially responsible utilities and industrials against the Dow Jones average. Available for $75 annually from Good Money Publications, Inc., P.O. Box 363, Worcester, VT 05682; telephone: (800) 535-3551; fax: (802) 223-8949. Subscribers also receive the quarterly newsletter *Netback* and a free copy of *Investors Guide to Environmentally and Socially Screened Mutual Funds*.

Investing for a Better World. This Franklin Research Development Corporation newsletter focuses on specific topics, such as women and investing, and covers other general news related to the socially responsible investment industry. A one-year subscription is available for $29.95. Also available is "Franklin's Insight," an investment advisory service offering stock recommendations from socially responsible companies and commentary on broad social investment and economic developments ($195/yr). Contact Franklin Research and Development Corporation, 711 Atlantic Ave., 5th Floor, Boston, MA 02111; telephone: (800) 548-5684 or (617) 423-6655; fax (617) 482-6179.

4. The Council on Economic Priorities (CEP) is a nonprofit public interest research group dedicated to enhancing corporate responsibility as it affects society through military spending, fair employment practices, community relations, and environmental impact. CEP provides investors with in-depth analyses of major corporations, focusing on social and environmental performance. For more information about its SCREEN program for investors, contact the Council on Economic Priorities, 30 Irving Place, New York, NY 10003-2386; telephone: (800) 729-4CEP or (212) 420-1133; fax: (212) 420-0988.

5. First Affirmative Financial Network in Colorado is a group of socially and environmentally aware stockbrokers offering investment services. For more information, contact First Affirmative Financial Network, 1040 S. 8th St., Suite 200, Colorado Springs, CO 80906; (800) 422-7284 or (719) 636-1045.

Action 96

Shareholder Activism

Why invest in companies that are antithetical to your value system? Because sometimes the only way to make changes is from the inside. As a shareholder, even if you own only one share, you are privy to information about the direction a company is moving in, as well as the time, place, and agenda for the annual shareholder meeting. Shareholder activists have been effective in influencing other stockholders to join them to pressure company officers to change destructive practices.

In 1971 the Episcopal Church made business history when it boldly filed the first church-sponsored shareholder resolution calling on General Motors to divest of its holdings in South Africa. The corporate responsibility movement has grown to include more than 220 Roman Catholic orders, dioceses, and pension funds and over 20 Protestant denominations, agencies, dioceses, and pension funds. Investments by these organizations collectively total more than $450 billion. Their investment strategies are coordinated by the Interfaith Center on Corporate Responsibility.

Some shareholder actions raise awareness; others lead to major changes. When Whirlpool was identified by the Council on Economic Priorities as one of a number of household companies involved in weapons manufacturing, a grassroots group in Los Angeles called Another Mother for Peace launched a massive letter-writing campaign calling on consumers to boycott the company until it ceased making weapons parts. Whirlpool terminated its military contracts as a result of the campaign.

What You Can Do

1. Read and vote on all corporate proxies you receive.
2. First Affirmative Financial Network has a shareholder activism program that connects individuals with institutional investors and coalitions that are sponsoring resolutions on hot issues. To learn more, contact First Affirmative Financial Network, 1040 S. 8th St., Suite 200, Colorado Springs, CO 80906; (800) 422-7284 or (719) 636-1045.
3. The Investor Responsibility Research Center offers proxy reports on social policy shareholder resolutions and an annual survey of institutions' votes and policies on shareholder resolutions. For information, contact the center at 1350 Connecticut Ave., NW, Suite 700, Washington, DC 20036; telephone: (202) 833-0700; fax: (202) 833-3555.
4. The Interfaith Center on Corporate Responsibility is the coordinating body for religious organizations wishing to invest responsibly. Contact it at 475 Riverside Drive, Room 566, New York, NY 10115; (212) 870-2936.

Part VII

The Responsible Consumer

Buying your way into a better world through ethical services, responsible businesses, constructive trade, and socially responsible travel

Chapter 28

Responsible Business: Redefining the Bottom Line

Business is no longer what it used to be. Led by a growing group of corporate visionaries and entrepreneurial heroes (yes, we have some—but not nearly enough), America is discovering that personal values and social ethics can be successfully combined with reasonable profit.

> Levi Strauss & Co., the world's largest clothing manufacturer, purchases much of its clothing from contractors in developing countries. Consistent with its commitment to good working conditions, this San Francisco company has adopted ground-breaking "Terms of Engagement" for all of its contractors. These guidelines include environmental requirements, ethical standards, health and safety codes, and employment practices.
>
> A dramatic example of the implementation of Levi Strauss' Terms of Engagement occurred when the company moved to terminate a contract with a manufacturer in Bangladesh because it employed child labor. Levi Strauss

Sources for this section include CEP *Research Reports* and SCREEN reports, and Mary Scott, "Not Business as Usual," *Business Ethics,* May/June 1994 (Minneapolis, MN).

learned that the child laborers were the only source of income for their families. They would likely resort to begging or prostitution if fired, or their families might starve. Levi Strauss insisted that the contractor pay the children full wages and benefits while they go to school. When they turn 14, they can opt for full time employment with the contractor. Levi Strauss is paying for their tuition, textbooks, and uniforms.*

Closer to home, former fashion designer Michael Sykes is using his business savvy to improve the lives of Los Angeles gang members. In the wake of the riots that ravaged his hometown, Sykes gave up his lucrative business and joined forces with Father Greg Boyle, a Jesuit priest who had called on business leaders to focus on local economic development. Soon after, Homeboy Industries, a neighborhood bakery, sprang into existence.

Sykes now spends his days supervising the rival gang members who proudly produce and package gourmet breads for specialty stores in Los Angeles. More than just a small business, this nonprofit bakery is a ticket to a new life for the gang members who work there. As Frank Rangel, once a member of the Mob Crew gang, says, "No one in my family thought I would succeed. I'm making five dollars per hour here, and even though selling drugs brought in more money, this is better. We're not chased by police. We don't have to stay up all night. We want the business to grow, so we can each have our own crew and get more homeboys off the streets."

Tom's of Maine is yet another company that combines social values with a strong bottom line. At a time when many businesses were reeling from recession, Tom's was enlarging its workforce to keep up with demand and donating 10 percent of pretax profits to charity. The company encourages employees to spend 5 percent of their work time volunteering with nonprofit organizations

*Excerpted with permission from the CEP *Research Report,* March/April 1994. For more information about CEP, see Action 99.

and offers excellent benefits, including generous parenting leave for both mothers and fathers. Concern for the environment has led Tom's to introduce a peat moss and gravel filtering system to strain out toothpaste residue from wastewater and improved packaging, like refillable glass roll-on deodorant containers. These are just a sample of the hundreds of stories that show that businesses really are beginning to redefine the bottom line.

Action 97

Shopping for a Better World

Purchasing General Electric light bulbs supports the nation's fourth largest defense contractor in its lobbying of the government for greater defense spending. Purchasing 3M products supports innovative pollution prevention programs. Every product you buy is a vote for the company that made it. By purchasing from companies whose policies are socially, ethically, and environmentally responsible, you can support your vision of how to make the world a better place. Or—unknowingly—you can support corporations that are pursuing a path that causes pain, war, social injustice, and environmental degradation.

As a consumer you have the power to:

✔ buy a camera from a company that stopped selling to South Africa because it did not want to support apartheid;

✔ purchase a breakfast cereal made by a company that pledges a generous 2 percent of its pretax earnings to charity;

✔ cook your supper on a kitchen range made by a company that is not involved in the manufacturing of nuclear weapons;

✔ snack on peanut butter made by one of the first major U.S. corporations to institute a comprehensive child-care network for its employees;

✔ invest in companies that have supported the advancement of women and minorities in management; and

✔ avoid buying from corporations whose policies you feel reflect a disregard for the public good.*

Ben & Jerry's, the Gap, Levi Strauss, Reebok, 3M, Tom's of Maine, and hundreds of other companies are turning handsome profits while valuing their employees, caring for the environment, supporting social change, and redefining the way America does business in the process.

But while more and more companies are seeing the value of developing a social and ecological conscience, others are dragging their feet. For example, take Rockwell International, a company maintaining a stone wall against public accountability. In 1992, the company was fined $18.5 million for environmental violations at the Rocky Flats nuclear weapons complex in Colorado. The company, once again under investigation for its conduct at the Colorado site, maintains that it no longer has a responsibility for cleaning up the damage it caused at Rocky Flats since its contract to operate the site ended in 1991. It was also the only company on CEP's list of the nation's top polluters in 1992 that refused to meet with CEP to discuss improving their record.

In the end, it's consumers who make the difference. Consumer support for what Ben & Jerry's terms "caring capitalism" can influence business to change for the better, but only if we can sort out the genuinely responsible from those who merely market themselves that way.

What You Can Do

The following resources can help you make informed buying decisions based on the social and environmental records of hundreds of different businesses.

*Excerpted with permission from Lyndenberg, Marlin, and Strub, *Rating America's Corporate Conscience* (Reading, MA: Addison-Wesley).

1. Businesses for Social Responsibility (BSR) is an independent, nonprofit organization that seeks to foster socially responsible corporate policies by bringing to the business community a unique perspective and resources that address the complex problems and enormous opportunities confronting both companies and society. There are more than seven hundred members and affiliates, each of which must be approved by the BSR board of directors. For information about BSR and the BSR Education Fund, which researches and disseminates information on corporate responsibility, contact BSR at 1030 15th St., NW, Suite 1010, Washington, DC 20005; telephone: (202) 842-5400; fax: (202) 842-3135. Below is a partial list of BSR members and other great businesses that are committed to being socially responsible.

Aveda
Ben & Jerry's
Blue Fish Clothing Company
The Body Shop, U.S.A.
Bright Horizons Children's Centers
Calvert Group
Esprit
Hanna Anderson
Just Desserts
Levi Strauss & Company
Odwalla
Patagonia
Quad/Graphics
Reebok International
Rhino Records
Rodale Press
Seeds of Change
Seventh Generation
Shaman Pharmaceuticals
Shorebank Corporation
Springfield Remanufacturing Corporation

Stonyfield Farms
Stride Rite Corporation
Tom's of Maine
Utne Reader
Veryfine Products
Working Assets Funding Service
Whole Foods Market

2. The Coalition for Environmentally Responsible Economics (CERES) is a nonprofit membership organization comprised of leading socially responsible investors, major environmental organizations, public pensions, labor and religious organizations, and public interest groups, including the National Audubon Society, the National Wildlife Federation, the Sierra Club, the Social Investment Forum, Interfaith Center on Corporate Responsibility, U.S. Public Interest Research Group, and the AFL-CIO Industrial Union Department.

CERES promotes responsible economic activity for a just, safe, and sustainable future throughout the world. By bringing together the corporate, environmental, and investment communities, it is working to change our patterns of behavior to reflect our belief that environmental protection and economic growth can go hand in hand. To that end it promotes the CERES Principles (formerly the Valdez Principles), a model corporate code of environmental conduct. A company that endorses the CERES Principles pledges to monitor and improve its behavior by protecting the biosphere through the sustainable use of natural resources, the reduction and disposal of wastes, energy conservation, risk reduction, safe products and services, and environmental restoration. Endorsing companies must back up these pledges with concrete information, reported annually in the *CERES Report,* which is made available to the public. For more information about becoming a friend of CERES, contact it at 711 Atlantic Ave., Boston, MA 02111; (617) 451-0927. To receive the CERES information kit, which includes the current guide to the CERES Principles, a complete list of signatories, the directory of CERES members, and a newsletter, include $5 with your inquiry. The annual environmental report is available for $250 (reduced rates available for coalition members and nonprofit organizations).

3. Avoid the recipients of the CEP's "Dirty Dozen" award, given to the country's biggest polluters. The 1993 recipients were:

Commonwealth Edison
E. I. du Pont de Nemours
Exxon Corporation
General Electric Company
International Paper Company
Louisiana-Pacific
Maxxam
Rockwell International
Texaco Inc.
Texas Utilities

4. Two of the best books to help you put your dollars in line with your values are *Shopping for a Better World* and *Students Shopping for a Better World*. Both books, produced by the CEP (see Action 99 for more information), rate manufacturers of clothing, food, computers, cosmetics, and other consumer products on issues like environmental responsibility, advancement of women and minorities, military contracts, charitable giving, animal testing, community outreach, and family benefits. Available from CEP, 30 Irving Place, New York, NY 10003-2386; (800) 729-4CEP. Call for price information on the latest editions of *Shopping for a Better World* and *Students Shopping for a Better World*.

5. Reading the following publications is an excellent way to keep up with the business practices of large and small cor-

porations. Contact the publishers for subscription information.

Business Ethics
52 10th St.
Suite 110
Minneapolis, MN 55403
(612) 962-4700

The Conscious Consumer Newsletter
P.O. Box 51
Wauconda, IL 60084
(708) 526-0522

The Green Business Letter
1526 Connecticut Ave., NW
Washington, DC 20036
(800) 955-4733

Action 98

Worker and Consumer Cooperatives

Here's how you can help support American workers support themselves. Here's your opportunity to do business with people who care, because they own the business. Here's your chance to encourage participation and responsibility rather than businesses who train their workers to say "it's not my job."

Cooperatives operate for the benefit of member-owners. In a cooperative, those with similar needs act together and pool their resources for mutual gain. The returns are not just monetary. Members ensure that their cooperative business provides the best-quality products and services at the lowest possible cost. Members control the business through an elected board of directors. Through their own participation, members extend the democratic practice into their own economic lives.

Nearly sixty million people have organized forty thousand U.S. cooperatives to provide themselves with goods and services in nearly every sector of our economy.

Consumer-owned cooperatives are owned by their members and enable them to secure a wide array of goods and services. For example, they may offer health care, utilities, insurance, or housing. They may buy and sell food, heating fuel, hardware, and other consumer goods. Or they may operate credit unions, funeral and memorial societies, or child-care facilities. Almost all consumer needs can be met by a cooperative.*

What You Can Do

To support worker-owned cooperatives, contact the Industrial Cooperative Association (ICA) for a list of more than eight hundred worker-owned cooperatives, divided by type of product and service and geographical location, so you can support cooperative businesses in your town or city. Lists can be ordered for $2 from ICA, 20 Park Plaza, Suite 1127, Boston, MA 02116; (617) 338-0010.

ICA puts out publications and provides workshops, technical assistance, and financing for worker cooperatives and employee-owned businesses.

Another helpful resource is *Cooperative Enterprise,* published quarterly and available at no charge from the National Cooperative Bank, 1401 I St., NW, Suite 700, Washington, DC 20005; (202) 336-7700.

For information on how to join a cooperative in your community, contact:

The National Cooperative Business Association (NCBA)
1401 New York Ave., NW, Suite 1100
Washington, DC 20005

*Exerpted from "Cooperatives Are . . .," by the National Cooperative Business Institute.

(202) 638-6222
Its publication Finding Co-ops: A Resource Guide and Directory *(1983), will help you find producer and consumer cooperatives nationwide. NCBA also provides material on how to start a variety of co-ops and buying clubs, as well as material on the history of the co-op movement and inspirational models such as Mondragón in Spain.*

North American Students of Cooperation (NASCO)
P.O. Box 7715
Ann Arbor, MI 48107
(313) 663-0889
NASCO has an excellent publications department and goes out of its way to answer questions and suggest resources.

Action 99

Support the Watchdog

The Council on Economic Priorities (CEP) is a public service research organization dedicated to accurate and impartial analysis of the social and environmental records of corporations. Since 1969, it has encouraged businesses and government to improve their records on environmental and social issues—with impressive results.

In 1970, CEP's environmental study of pollution controls at the largest pulp and paper manufacturers resulted in the installation of pollution-control equipment and demonstrable improvements within two years. The 1981 publication of *The Politics of Defense Contracting: The Iron Triangle* led to a Department of Defense prohibition against billing lobbying costs to DOD contracts.

Congressional testimony, educational campaigns, and the publication of *Building a Peace Economy* in 1990 culminated in a law that provided $200 million in federal aid to help communities cope with cuts in defense spending and set the precedent for more substantial conversion programs since 1990.

CEP continues to be at the forefront of social activism, working with businesses and empowering consumers, investors, managers, employees, and activists to cast their economic vote as conscientiously as their political vote. The cover of one of their publications features words from Disraeli: "As a general rule, the most successful people in life are those who have the best information." CEP's information is some of the best available anywhere.

What You Can Do

CEP offers a wealth of information to help you make more informed decisions, whether you're buying, investing, or demanding change. Individual membership in CEP is just $25 a year; members receive a copy of *Shopping for a Better World* (see Action 97) as well as quarterly research reports. For more information, contact CEP at 30 Irving Place, New York, NY 10003-2386; (800) 729-4CEP.

Action 100
Boycotts

Boycotts offer consumers another way to cast their vote against irresponsible corporate behavior every time they step up to the cash register.

Consumer boycotts are organized programs designed to place financial pressure on a corporation to change a given policy. Some boycotts have lasted years and become well known, such as the boycott of Nestlé to protest the use of its infant formula in Third World countries. But there are hundreds of smaller, local, and less publicized boycotts going on at any one time. They've included those against:

- ✔ *California table grapes,* organized by the United Farm Workers of America against pesticide use in the fields
- ✔ *State of Colorado,* in response to the passage of Amendment 2, which prevents the passage of laws that would allow gays and lesbians special minority privileges
- ✔ *Hormel,* organized by union workers to protest wage cuts and unsafe working conditions

✔ *Scott Paper*, for its harmful forestry practices and its destruction of the rain forest
✔ *Morton Salt* (a division of Morton Thiokol), to protest its role as a top nuclear weapons contractor
✔ *Norway*, for its plans to resume commercial whaling in defiance of the International Whaling Commission ban

Boycotts are a simple way for you to play an active role in supporting issues that concern you most, and they allow you to cast your vote against a corporate practice that you find offensive.

What You Can Do

Boycott Action News
Co-op America
1850 M Street, NW
Suite 700
Washington, DC 20036
Telephone: (202) 872-5307
Fax: (202) 872-5202
Boycott Action News *is a feature of the* Co-op America
Quarterly *and lists on going and new boycotts. The publication is free to members or can be ordered for $20/yr.*

Boycott Quarterly
Center for Economic Democracy
P.O. Box 64
Olympia, WA 98507-0064
This 68-page quarterly is full of interesting articles, as well as an extensive listing of who's being boycotted and why. $20 a year for four issues.

INFACT: Campaigning for Corporate Accountability
256 Hanover St.
Boston, MA 02113
Telephone: (617) 742-4583

Fax: (617) 367-0191

INFACT is a grassroots organization that organizes national boycotts of the country's worst environmental offenders. It publishes a quarterly newsletter, INFACT Update, *that provides in-depth coverage of its current boycotts and provides you with innovative ways to become involved.*

Chapter 29

Ethical Services: Credit Cards, Long-Distance Phone Calls, Insurance and Travel

Action 101
Working Assets Credit Card

The Working Assets VISA card advertises itself quite aggressively as the first *socially responsible credit card*. After you become a cardholder and make your first purchase, Working Assets contributes $2 to a nonprofit organization working for peace, human rights, the environment, or the hungry. Then, every time you make a purchase using your card, an additional five cents is contributed to the same groups working to help change the world. In 1993 alone, Working Assets customers generated more than $1 million for thirty-six groups, including Greenpeace, Planned Parenthood, Amnesty International, and Oxfam America. Each year customers get to nominate their favorite

Sources for this section include EcoNet Green Travel Forum (cdp:green.travel); *EcoTraveler*, March/April 1994; "Working Vacations," *Outdoor Magazine*, June 1994 (Chicago, IL).

nonprofit organization and vote on how to distribute the money that's accumulating in the Working Assets donation pool.

Working Assets also provides cardholders with an easy and effective way to speak out to political and corporate leaders. Your monthly statement will include timely information on issues like gun control, health care, and wilderness preservation. For a low fee, Working Assets will send a well-argued "CitizenLetter" on your behalf to the targeted decision maker.

The Working Assets credit card offers many benefits, including no annual fee for the first year; an initial credit line of up to $5,000 for the "classic card" and $20,000 for the "gold card"; a variable annual percentage rate; a 25-day period to pay amounts due before interest starts accruing; cash advances at 40,000 Cirrus ATMs nationwide; bills printed on recycled paper; and more. To date, Working Assets has more than 75,000 cardholders helping to make the world a better place.

What You Can Do

Call Working Assets' toll-free number for a credit card application: (800) 522-7759.

Action 102

The Responsible Way to Make Long-Distance Phone Calls

With Working Assets Long Distance, you can help the same progressive groups supported by the Working Assets credit card—*at no extra cost to you.* Every time you make a call on its long-distance network, it puts 1 percent of your charge in a donation pool for nonprofit groups working to save the rain forest, house the homeless, defend reproductive rights, and more.

In 1993, more than $1 million was donated to thirty-six nonprofit groups fighting for social, environmental, and economic change. And every year, customers help select the groups that Working Assets funds.

Working Assets uses phone lines from one of the major carriers so you get easy direct dialing, clear fiber-optic sound, direct international calling, and twenty-four-hour operations. Its basic interstate rates are guaranteed to be low because it buys network time in bulk.

Long-distance customers can also speak out on vital issues. On each phone bill (which is printed on 100 percent post-consumer recycled paper), Working Assets gives the names and phone numbers of key political and business leaders to contact. You can call these leaders on any "Monday-Free Speech Day," and Working Assets pays for the call. Other days you get a 25 percent "citizenship discount." If you'd rather express your opinion in writing, you can check a box on your bill, and Working Assets will send a CitizenLetter in your name. Since 1988, Working Assets customers influenced public policy with more than 600,000 calls and letters.

What You Can Do

To sign up with Working Assets Long Distance or to request additional information, call (800) 788-8588.

Here are two more phone services you can call for information. Both of them donate a portion of your service fee to support environmental organizations.

Earth Tones: (800) 327-8456 or (617) 423-3103
LCI International's *Earthtalk:* (800) 860-1020 or (614) 798-6000

Action 103

Insurance Services

Until national health care becomes a reality in the United States, the decisions you make about your insurance coverage will continue to make a difference. Why? Because the premiums you pay (or your employer pays) to your insurance company are invested in a socially indiscriminate manner to yield the highest return for the insurance provider. In any given year, premiums paid in are likely to exceed claims. As long as this is the case, the insurance carrier uses the difference in whatever way it sees fit, which may include investing in liquor, tobacco, and oil companies or a corporation that endangers the lives of its workers through inadequate safety precautions. You have no control over how these premiums are invested and whether those investments are consistent with your values.

There is an alternative. By purchasing health insurance through Alternative Health Insurance Services (AHIS), you not only receive benefits for alternative and holistic health services but can be sure that a portion of your premiums is invested in financially secure community economic development banks that are working to build a more just and sustainable economy.

What You Can Do

1. For information on AHIS plans available in your area and a free rate quote, give AHIS a call at (800) 966-8467.
2. For information on socially responsible life insurance, contact First Affirmative Financial Network, Inc., 1040 S. 8th St., Suite 200, Colorado Springs, CO 80906; (800) 422-7284 or (719) 636-1045.

Action 104
Traveling with a Conscience

The reasons for travel are as varied as the destinations people choose, but our collective desire to roam the globe has made tourism the second largest export industry in the world, employing nearly 130 million people and generating $3.5 trillion a year. Clearly, travelers are making an impact worldwide.

Until recently the impact has tended to be associated with the gross overdevelopment of pristine environments, the upsetting of local cultures, and loud, insensitive tourists. This has been especially true in less developed countries. Not surprising, for more than five thousand tourists from industrialized countries set out on a Third World adventure every hour.

Tourism has become the leading source of income for many developing countries, yet this booming industry benefits them less than you might think. Tourist dollars often end up in the hands of large corporations, located in industrialized nations, that control most of the hotels, airlines, tour operators, and travel agencies. Native communities are pushed aside to make way for high-rise hotels and private beaches. Fishermen and fisherwomen, farmers, and craftspeople are turned into bartenders and hotel workers. Prostitution often becomes a new growth industry, and disease spreads quickly through local populations.

But the recent trend toward more socially and economically responsible travel is revolutionizing the industry. The new brand of travel—known as alternative tourism, socially responsible tourism, social tourism, or ecotourism—has gained tremendous momentum, and not just in the Third World. Today more than one hundred groups in the United States alone are organizing alternative travel with an astounding range: bicycle treks through China, freighter trips through Labrador, peace tours to the Pacific Islands, socially conscious pilgrimages to the Holy Land, locally run village resorts in West Africa, and environmentally responsible beach resorts in Bali.

Princess Cruise Lines, one of the largest travel companies in the world, recently invested $10 million to equip its ships with waste management technology and now has a full-time vice president of environmental health programs.

Indigenous people in Borneo, in the face of government-sanctioned destruction of traditional hunting grounds, are using the popularity of ecotourism to save their rain forest–based culture. Endorsed by the Rainforest Action Network and other groups, the Penan Guide Project allows visitors the rare opportunity to join the nomadic Penan people on hunting and gathering expeditions.

The American Society of Travel Agents (ASTA, 1101 King St., Alexandria, VA 22314; [703] 739-2782) is taking a proactive approach to ecotourism, encouraging agents and tourists alike to adhere to the following guidelines:

ASTA's Ten Commandments on Eco-Tourism

1. Respect the frailty of the Earth. Realize that unless all are willing to help in its preservation, unique and beautiful destinations may not be here for future generations to enjoy.
2. Leave only footprints. Take only photographs. No graffiti. No litter. Do not take away souvenirs from historical sites and natural areas.
3. To make your travel more meaningful, educate yourself about the geography, customs, manners and culture of the region you visit. Take time to listen to the people. Encourage local conservation efforts.
4. Respect the privacy and dignity of others. Inquire before photographing people.
5. Do not buy products made from endangered plants or animals, such as ivory, tortoise shell, animal skins and feathers. Read "Know Before You Go," the U.S. Customs list of products which cannot be imported.
6. Always follow designated trails. Do not disturb animals, plants or their natural habitats.
7. Learn about and support conservation-oriented programs and organizations working to preserve the environment.
8. Whenever possible, walk or utilize environmentally-sound methods of transportation. Encourage drivers of public vehicles to stop engines when parked.
9. Patronize those (hotels, airlines, resorts, cruise lines, tour operators and suppliers) who advance energy and environmental conservation; water and air quality; recycling; safe management of waste and toxic materials; noise abatement; community involvement; and which provide experienced, well trained staff dedicated to strong principles of conservation.
10. Ask ASTA travel agents to identify organizations which

subscribe to ASTA Environmental Guidelines for air, land and sea travel. ASTA has recommended that these organizations adopt their own environmental codes to cover special sites and ecosystems.*

What You Can Do

1. There are currently no regulations governing the use of terms like "eco-tourism," nor has any watchdog organization emerged to help tourists ferret out companies making false or misleading claims. The best thing to do is ask a lot of questions of any travel company you are thinking of doing business with: What is their mission? What steps do they take to prevent pollution and preserve the natural and social landscape as much as possible? It's also a good idea to ask for the names of a few people who have been on past tours.

2. The best bet for information on the ecotravel industry is the Ecotourism Society, whose mission is to increase the implementation of ecotourism principles and practices around the world. Membership is $15 for students; $35 for individuals, which includes a free copy of "The New Ethic in Adventure Travel." Professional and Institutional memberships are also available. For more information, contact the Ecotourism Society, P.O. Box 755 Bennington, VT 05257-0755; (802) 447-2121.

3. A good source of information on travel destinations is *EcoTraveler* magazine. You'll also find advertisement in the magazine useful for learning about different tour companies. Published bimonthly by Skies America Publishing Company, a year's subscription is $36. For more information, contact *EcoTraveler* magazine at Skies America Publishing Co., 9560 S.W. Nimbus Ave., Beaverton, OR 97008; telephone: (503) 520-1955; fax: (503) 520-1275. Other good periodicals to consider are:

*Reprinted with permission from the American Society of Travel Agents.

Great Expeditions Magazine
P.O. Box 18036
Raleigh, NC 27619
(919) 846-3600
Focuses on creating a network of socially responsible travelers.

Kokopelli Notes
Dept. NGP
P.O. Box 8186
Asheville, NC 28814
(704) 683-4844
Explores ways in which travel choices impact the earth; encourages walking and bicycling.

Transitions Abroad
18 Hulst Rd.
P.O. Box 344
Amherst, MA 01004-1300
(413) 256-0373
Focuses on socially responsible travel.

4. A popular form of socially conscious adventure is volunteer vacations. Run by organizations such as Earthwatch ([800]776-0188) and the University Research Expeditions Program of the University of California at Berkeley ([510] 642-6586) these trips allow individuals to do valuable work, ranging from research to trail maintenance, while visiting off-the-beaten-trail locations they might never have access to otherwise. Some good publications to look at are:

Environmental Vacations, by Stephanie Ocko. Available from John Muir Publications: (800) 888-7504.
Helping Out in the Outdoors. Published by the American Hiking Society: (703) 255-9304.
Volunteer Vacations, by Bill McMillon. Available from Chicago Review Press: (312) 337-0747.

5. A great way to travel if you really want to meet people is through Servas, Inc. This international network matches travelers with host families who welcome visitors for short stays. If you are planning a trip or are interested in being a host, contact Servas at 11 John St., #407, New York, NY 10038; telephone: (212) 267-0252; fax: (212) 267-0292.

Part VIII

Peace, Justice, and Social Change

A fresh look at ways to combat problems of discrimination, prejudice, and human rights abuses with letters, phone calls, and increased awareness of your own beliefs and attitudes

Chapter 30

Why Are So Many People Treating Social Change like a Spectator Sport?

Since Bill Clinton took office, there has been an unnerving decline in peace and justice movements nationwide.

America's crises have hardly eased. Yet countless individuals once on the front lines of social change now seem stuck on the sidelines. Instead of becoming involved in urgent campaigns, they watch from a distance, following political events on NPR or CNN, casting judgment on each twist and turn, much as if they were following the fortunes of a baseball team.

Opportunities for change exist, if we will only pursue them. The popular mood is volatile and confused. The President swings like a weather vane with each new shift he perceives. Yet, even this waffling opens major opportunities. In a period of equivalent social crisis, Franklin Roosevelt did not enact his pivotal New Deal reforms until he was significantly pushed. John Kennedy was dragged and pressured by grassroots movements into eventual support for major civil rights legislation.

But change won't happen automatically. We need to ask what we want in this nation and why: how we should run our economy, meet human needs, protect the Earth, achieve greater justice. Real answers to these questions probably won't be spearheaded by the President, though he might follow if others lead. They have to come from us, as we reach out to listen and learn, engage fellow citizens who aren't currently involved, and spur debate in environments that are habitually silent.*

We hope the issues covered in this section—racial prejudice, human rights, abuses, and discrimination—will inspire you to action. Every small step you take in combating these problems moves us all one step closer to a more peaceful and secure world.

Paul Rogat Loeb, *Generation at the Crossroads*, ©1994 by Paul Rogat Loeb. Reprinted by permission of Rutgers University Press.

Chapter 31

Promoting World Peace

Action 105
Amnesty International: Your Letter May Help Set Someone Free

Amnesty International works tirelessly, through supporters around the world, to help set free men, women, and children who are being illegally imprisoned and tortured for crimes ranging from practicing the wrong religion to being born the wrong color, speaking out against oppression, even speaking the wrong language.

In 1993 prisoners of conscience were held in sixty-three countries, more than 100,000 political prisoners were locked up in detention without charge or trial in fifty-three countries, more than 112 governments tortured prisoners, and political killings by the state took place in sixty-one countries. The death penalty was carried out on approximately 2,000 people in thirty-three countries.

In a world of rapid political change, human rights groups have sprung up in dozens of countries where they could not have operated freely before. But the new freedoms, and those who defend them, are in danger in countries teetering on the brink of crisis and violence. Human rights defenders—lawyers, journalists, trade unionists, peasant leaders, and many others—are playing a key role in countries going through major transitions and reforms, by helping to establish legal and constitutional safeguards for human rights and creating a safe space for peaceful dissent. But human rights defenders often become the first victims of governments trying to build a good human rights image abroad and fearful of the damage activists can do to that image.

Here's a brief overview of the problems Amnesty International worked to alleviate worldwide in 1993. These and many similar injustices continue today.

Europe: In Bosnia and Herzegovina, hundreds of deliberate and arbitrary killings by all sides were reported. At least 15,000 people, many of them prisoners of conscience, were held in detention camps during the conflict.

In twenty-six other countries in Europe, including France, Italy, Portugal, Spain, Turkey, and the Federal Republic of Yugoslavia, there were reports of torture or ill-treatment in prisons, police stations, or other detention centers. At least twenty-four people in Turkey died in custody, apparently as a result of torture, a practice reportedly widespread among Turkish police. Many victims were human rights defenders.

In some countries that emerged from the breakup of the former Soviet Union, authorities promised new rights that their security forces then suppressed. In Tadzhikistan, extrajudicial executions and "disappearances" continued, killing scores of people targeted for their political activities or regional origins. In Turkmenistan, authorities jailed opponents to prevent meetings with foreign dignitaries.

Middle East: In the Middle East, human rights activists faced criticism. For example, Mansur Kikhiya, a prominent opponent of Libya's government and a founding member of the Arab Organization for Human Rights, "disappeared" in Egypt following his reported abduction by Libyan government agents.

There were widespread arbitrary arrests of thousands who were suspected of opposing the government or sympathizing with Islamic groups in Algeria, Egypt, Iraq, and Tunisia. Prisoners of conscience were held in eleven countries, including Egypt, Iran, Israel, and the Occupied Territories.

Americas: In 1993, Amnesty International launched an international campaign against political killings and "disappearances," violations that claimed more than a thousand lives across some fifteen countries in the Americas, including Brazil, El Salvador, Guatemala, Haiti, and Peru. In Colombia, for example, the armed forces and their paramilitary agents executed hundreds of people. Hundreds of prisoners of conscience were held in several countries, including Peru and Cuba. In Brazil, hundreds of street children, adolescents, and adults were killed or disappeared. Torture and ill-treatment by police were widely reported in many countries, including Haiti, Venezuela, Mexico, Peru, and Colombia.

Africa: In Africa, political killings were the predominant human rights violation, though political arrests and torture continued in 1993. Foreshadowing the violence in Rwanda in 1994, tens of thousands of people died in Burundi as local Hutu government officials and supporters killed Tutsi civilians, while Tutsi groups and security forces also killed thousands of unarmed Hutu civilians. Hundreds of extrajudicial executions and disappearances were also reported in twenty countries, including Angola, Chad, Liberia, Rwanda, Senegal, Togo, and Zaire.

Asia: In Asia, extrajudicial executions and disappearances continued to be widespread across the region. Hundreds of extrajudicial executions were reported in Cambodia as well as in Afghanistan, where deliberate and indiscriminate bombings of homes, hospitals, and mosques also left hundreds dead and thousands injured. In India, hundreds of political activists were extrajudicially executed and scores more were "disappeared" by security forces in the states of Jammu and Kashmir and of Punjab. In Pakistan, hundreds of people were reportedly tortured by police or in military custody, in some cases resulting in death.

Torture and ill-treatment of political detainees, peaceful protesters, and criminal suspects were common in nineteen Asian countries, including China and Indonesia, where hundreds of suspected government opponents, were prisoners of conscience or possible prisoners of conscience. In Myanmar hundreds of government opponents, including dozens of prisoners of conscience, remained imprisoned. The death penalty was imposed in at least ten countries. In China alone, more than 1,400 people were executed and more than 2,500 remained sentenced to death.

What You Can Do

Join Amnesty in its fight to release political prisoners and oppose human rights abuses around the world. To become a member, send whatever you can (suggested membership fee is $25, $16 for students and seniors). Write to National Office, Amnesty International USA, 322 8th Ave., New York, NY 10001; (212) 807-8400.

Action 106

Promoting a Domestic Agenda for Peace: Peace Action

The fact is that true peace and security can come only from a healthy economy and a demilitarized global environment. Peace Action is working at a grassroots level to refocus national attention on issues that promote peace and stability in this country and worldwide.

Formerly called SANE/FREEZE, Peace Action is a membership organization that works through national and grassroots citizens' action to stress not only peace-oriented domestic priorities but also an immediate end to nuclear weapons testing, abolition of the arms trade, and complete global disarmament. It works to reduce significantly spending for unnecessary military and weapons programs and to foster increased investment in health, education, and renewal projects like transportation and housing.

Each year Peace Action brings its message to 1.5 million people in forty states though door-to-door visits, on the phone, through the mail, and in public meetings. It also lobbies for policy changes in Congress, state capitals, city halls, and the United Nations. The organization prepares a weekly hotline on current federal legislation and publishes an annual voting record for every member of Congress, and its education department disseminates information through videos, fact sheets, and radio spots.

What You Can Do

Become a member of Peace Action, and you will:

1. Gain access to an extensive peace legislative action network
2. Receive a quarterly newsletter with action projects relating to local, national, and international issues
3. Become a local member of the nearest Peace Action chapter (contact the national office for information)

Peace Action
National Office
1819 H St., NW
Suite 640
Washington, DC 20006
Telephone: (202) 862-9740
Fax: (202) 862-9762
E-mail: sfnatldc@igc.apc.org

Action 107

Postcards for Change: EarthAction Network

EarthAction is an international network of one thousand organizations from 125 countries. Its goal is to mobilize worldwide public pressure on governments and corporations to address problems that threaten the life of our planet. Launched at the Earth Summit in Rio de Janeiro, EarthAction enables individuals and organizations from every corner of the planet to act together on global issues of common concern.

The strategy of EarthAction is adapted from Amnesty International. Every month each of the one thousand partner organizations in the network receives an "EarthAction Tool Kit" that is focused on one global issue and timed to coincide with a major event or international decision being made. Each tool kit includes an "action alert," with brief background information on the current issue, and a recommended action—usually to send a message via phone, mail, or fax to a policy maker facing a critical decision on that issue. The tool kit also includes a sample action letter, press release, and letter to the editor for use with local media.

Every three months, EarthAction focuses on one environmental, one developmental, and one peace issue. Individual members and partner organizations agree to take action at least four times a year on the EarthAction issues that interest them. As a result of these coordinated actions, policy makers throughout the world receive clear and timely messages from citizens about global concerns. Simultaneously, these issues are spotlighted in the press the world over.

Alerts to date have dealt with ozone depletion; the wars in Bosnia, Mozambique, Somalia, and Sudan; strengthening the UN; protecting the temperate rain forest in British Columbia; reducing the ongoing threat posed by nuclear weapons; restructuring the World Bank; demarcating indigenous lands in Brazil; and the issues of population and consumption.

Organizations from developing countries can become net-

258

work members at no charge; those from more affluent countries are asked to contribute between $30 and $100 annually. Individuals may subscribe directly to EarthAction for an annual membership fee of $25. For information or to join EarthAction, write, call, or fax the office nearest you.

EarthAction
30 Cottage St.
Amherst, MA 01002
Telephone: (413) 549-8118
Fax: (413) 549-0544
E-mail: earthaction@igc.apc.org

Chapter 32

Citizen Diplomacy

The New Age of Diplomacy and Foreign Policy

Thousands of ordinary citizens have reached out across political, ideological, geographic, and governmental barriers to form relationships that will encourage peace, understanding, and partnership. Their initiatives have given birth to a new age of diplomacy and foreign policy and created new opportunities to engage in meaningful relationships with people around the world.

The following actions will explore your options as an individual citizen diplomat.

Action 108

How to Become a Citizen Diplomat

In a world of excessive military expenditures, nuclear overkill, endless civil wars, unrest, and international terrorism—diplomacy can clearly not be left to diplomats.

Global problems have simply become too complex to be

solved by just a few national leaders. If we ever hope to deal with these problems effectively, we will need to harness the ideas, skills, and goodwill of many of the world's five billion "unofficial" leaders—people like ourselves. Thomas Jefferson once wrote that "the good sense of the people will always be found to be the best army." If more of us were involved in global problem solving, we could begin to find more common ground on which to work together and more nonviolent ways to tolerate and reconcile our differences.

Just as diplomats facilitate communication between governments, you, as a "citizen diplomat," can facilitate communication among the world's inhabitants. The more contact you have with people in other countries through meetings, letters, visits, lectures, electronic bulletin boards, and cultural exchanges, the more you can help everyone recognize that they are all more than Americans, Chinese, Bosnians, or North Koreans—they are international citizens with a common stake in survival.

Citizen diplomacy won't eliminate global conflict overnight; nothing can do that. But it can begin transforming violent, nation-versus-nation conflicts into nonviolent debates over specific issues. As long as the world's controversies are framed territorially—North Korea vs. South Korea, Serbia vs. Bosnia—arms races and wars will remain and proliferate. But if international coalitions nourished through citizen diplomacy coalesce among the world's developers, environmentalists, urbanites, farmers, workers, peace advocates, business people, and leaders, controversies will increasingly be defined in political, not geographic, terms. Once we find ourselves agreeing with people from other countries on some issues and disagreeing on others, we can begin to see possibilities for true understanding. The more empathy we have for foreigners, the less likely we will kill them—and the less likely they will want to destroy us. Only then will we begin finding lasting solutions to the world's problems.*

What You Can Do

Become a host family for a foreign student or Servas traveler (see below); stay with a Servas host when you travel; strike up a conversation with backpack-toting visitors to your town; or start conversations with people around the globe via the Internet (see Action 31). Developing personal relationships with people from other countries is one of the best ways to become a citizen diplomat. Not only are you able to share your perspective, but you get an unfiltered view of what is happening in other parts of the world. Here are some organizations that can help you build your own bridges:

American Field Service (AFS)
40 Wall St., 47th Floor
New York, NY 10005
Telephone: (212) 344-6400
Fax: (212) 809-4872
AFS is one of the oldest and largest student exchange organizations. Contact it to find out how you can host a high school student from another country.

ISAR
1601 Connecticut Ave., NW
Suite 301
Washington, DC 20009
Telephone: (202) 387-3034
Fax: (202) 667-3291
E-mail: isar@igc.apc.org
Contact ISAR to learn how you can support citizen diplomacy in Eurasia. Founded in 1983, ISAR's mission was to reduce the threat of

*Excerpted with permission from Michael Shuman, *Having International Affairs Your Way,* produced by the Center for Innovative Diplomacy.

*nuclear confrontation between the United States and the Soviet Union
by building links between the people of both countries. In the post-Soviet
era ISAR works to support local initiatives and empower local citizens
seeking to create more just and sustainable societies in Eurasia.*

Parliamentarians for Global Action
211 E. 43d St.,
Suite 1604
New York, NY 10017
Telephone: (212) 687-7755
Fax: (212) 687-8409
*This organization works toward disarmament and a more just and
secure international system through a worldwide network of legislators.*

Partners of the Americas
1424 K St., NW
Suite 400
Washington, D.C. 20005
Telephone: (202) 628-3300
Fax: (202) 628-3306
E-mail: mt@partners.poa.com
*Contact Partners of the Americas to get involved with citizen diplomacy
in Latin America and the Caribbean. Partners was established in 1964
as a bridge between people in the United States and our neighbors to the
south. Its sixty partner members link thirty-one countries of Latin
America and the Caribbean with forty-five U.S. states and the District
of Columbia.*

Servas
11 John St., #407
New York, NY 10038
Telephone: (212) 267-0252
Fax: (212) 267-0292
*Servas is an international cooperative system of hosting travelers in
130 countries. Established in 1948, its mission is to help build world
peace, goodwill and understanding by providing opportunities for deeper, more personal contact among people of diverse cultures and back-*

grounds. Contact Servas for more information about becoming a host or a traveler.

Action 109

Sister Cities

In 1956 President Dwight Eisenhower presented the sister cities concept, and twenty years later Sister Cities International picked up on his initiative. From 1976 to 1994, Sister Cities matched 1,041 American cities with 1,608 cities in 113 countries. The program is firmly rooted in the ideal that we are all members of a single community that is global in scope and that no nation alone can hope to solve our most pressing problems. Time and time again, Sister Cities International has proven that when cities and individuals come together to share their ideas, cultures, and common problems, old misunderstandings and prejudices are replaced by a spirit of cooperation." Following are a few examples of the kinds of projects Sister Cities International has been involved with.

✔ Lawyers and city officials in Dallas, Texas, helped draft a new constitution for Latvia.
✔ Kansas City, Missouri, had an exhibit at Expo '92 in its sister city of Seville, Spain, showcasing its pioneer and jazz heritage to over 1.7 million international visitors.
✔ Jacksonville, Florida, has donated close to $1 million in medical supplies, equipment, and expert training to Murmansk, Russia.
✔ New Brunswick, New Jersey; Debrecen, Hungary; and Tsuruoka, Japan, are involved in a trilateral program that has each city working together to solve common urban problems such as waste management and its effects on the environment.
✔ A youth program in Omaha, Nebraska, and Braunschweig, Germany, is being set up to attack head-on one of the most troublesome problems facing many cities

today: the integration of ethnic minorities living in their communities.

These are only a few of the thousands of relationships that are building international understanding and laying the groundwork for more peaceful relations between countries.

What You Can Do

To find out how you can get involved, contact:

Sister Cities International
120 S. Payne St.
Alexandria, VA 22314
Telephone: (703) 836-3535
Fax: (703) 836-4815

Action 110

Weaving Your Way to Global Understanding: A Success Story

Peace Fleece is a business that was created out of one family's despair over the possibility of nuclear war. In the mid-1980s Peter Hagerty and his wife, Marty Tracy, who live in rural Maine and raise sheep for their wool, wondered daily "what was the purpose of raising all these lambs, growing all this feed, if all at once the sky could light up and everything we value could disappear?"

Their quest for more peaceful relations began with a vibrant connection between their small Maine farmstead and citizens in what was then the Soviet Union. Peter and Mary believed that creating a bridge of peace through personal relationships would begin to reduce the chances of war. Their solution was to purchase wool from Soviet farmers, blend it with their own, and market this Soviet-American wool to consumers along with knit-

265

ting patterns, instructions, and a booklet telling the story in Russian and English.

Since Peter and Mary received the first twelve-hundred-pound shipment from Krasnodar, a beautiful farm district that borders the Black Sea, many more shipments have arrived, and twenty-six colors of yarn are now available.

Peace Fleece still works with a small Moscow cooperative to produce hand-painted wooden knitting needles and buttons. The company is also opening an office in the former Central Asian Republic of Kirgizya, where high-quality merino wool is produced. In addition, it is working with a small group of Palestinian and Israeli shepherds to manufacture a line of multi-colored weaving yarns and spinning products.

What You Can Do

To receive a Peace Fleece catalog of mittens, hats, vests, cardigans, pullovers, knitting kits, and yarn sample card, send $2 to:

Peace Fleece
RFD 1, Box 57
Kezar Falls, ME 04047
Telephone: (207) 625-4906
Fax: (207) 625-3360

Action III

Resources for Peace: A Survey of Activist and Educational Organizations

American Friends Service Committee
Peace Education Division
1501 Cherry St.
Philadelphia, PA 19102
(215) 241-7000
This activist group works for peace, justice, and equality worldwide.

*Programs are based on the conviction that nonviolent solutions can be
found to problems.*

Children's Creative Response to Conflict
P.O. Box 271
Nyack, NY 10960
Telephone: (914) 353-1796
Fax: (914) 358-4924
*This organization assists students and teachers in carrying out activities
to allow children to examine conflicts and develop nonviolent solutions.*

Nonviolence International
P.O. Box 39127
Friendship Station, NW
Washington, DC 20016
Telephone: (202) 244-0951
Fax: (202) 244-6396
*The purpose of Nonviolence International is to provide assistance to
individuals, organizations, and governments seeking nonviolent means to
achieve their social and political goals.*

Peace Brigades International
2642 College Ave.
Berkeley, CA 94704
(510) 540-0749
*Peace Brigades provides a nonviolent, nonpartisan international presence
in situations of violent conflict or repression to support nonviolence,
human rights, and social justice efforts.*

Search for Common Ground
1601 Connecticut Ave., NW
Suite 200
Washington, DC 20009
Telephone: (202) 265-4300
Fax: (202) 232-6718
This organization promotes collaborative problem solving to divisive

national and international issues by channeling conflict toward win-win outcomes and, hence, to build a more secure and peaceful world.

To learn about the many other organizations that are working for world peace, contact Access. Ask how you can take advantage of its extensive database.

Access: A Security Information Service
1511 K St., NW
Suite 643
Washington, DC 20005
Telephone: (202) 783-6050
Fax: (202) 783-4767

Building Bridges to Better Understanding: Ending Racism, Discrimination, and Promoting Women's and Gay Rights

Despite the progress that has been made in the United States toward achieving racial justice since the civil rights movement, such social problems as poverty, unemployment, urban decay, deteriorating educational opportunities, crime, and violence are all aggravated by the persistence of racism in our society.

It is important that we keep moving forward with the necessary legal reforms to reduce racial and all forms of discrimination, but there is much truth in the saying that we can't legislate an end to racism, because that can begin only in the human heart. The struggle against racism must be carried forward not only in the courts and legislative bodies, but also in our personal relationships, in our places of work and worship, in schools, playgrounds, the media and in every institution of our society.

Martin Luther King, Jr., said that "like life, racial understanding is not something we find, but something that we must create . . . the ability to work together, to understand each other will not be found ready made, it must be created by the fact of contact."*

Action 112

Understanding Racism

While the effects of racism involve us all—people of color have been and remain the primary "targets" of racism. Racism shapes the lives of people of color through fear of physical harm, reduction of economic and social opportunities, and the psychological burden of being viewed as inferior. But we all suffer. As a nation racism diminishes the number of people contributing to our economic and social well-being. In our personal lives racism keeps us locked into a cycle of hatred, prejudice, and anger, and in simple human terms racism ignores, devalues, and degrades the wonderful diversity of our human family.

The goal of ending racism is to recognize, accept, include, honor, and celebrate the diversity of human beings. A "color-blind" or "melting-pot" society ignores the uniqueness and individuality of different people and groups. Instead, we can affirm "unity in diversity." The goal of ending racism is the certain knowledge that as people we are more similar than different. Our differences detract from no one, instead they benefit us all.

We needn't worry about where to start. Any step towards ending racism, regardless of how small, contributes to the larger journey we must take as families, communities, and nations.†

---

*Excerpted with permission from Clyde Ford, *We Can All Get Along: Fifty Steps You Can Take to Help End Racism* (New York: Dell, 1994).
†Ibid.

What You Can Do

1. Racism is, more than anything, a question of attitude. The first step is to examine your own feelings and prejudices with honesty. None of us is without prejudice. The recently erected Holocaust museum in Los Angeles makes the point this way: As visitors move through the exhibit, they are instructed to choose between two doors, one marked "prejudiced" and one "not prejudiced." Anyone choosing the "not prejudiced" door discovers that it is locked.

2. Since racism is a huge topic that we cannot begin to do justice to in this volume, we highly recommend you read *We Can All Get Along: Fifty Steps You Can Take to Help End Racism*, by Clyde Ford (New York: Dell, 1994). This excellent book goes to the heart of issues dividing ethnic groups and offers positive suggestions for action in areas ranging from raising children with nonracist beliefs to eliminating racism in housing, education, and health care.

3. The following groups are working to eliminate racism and counter its negative effects. Contact any of them to find out how you can get involved.

Three of the oldest organizations working to end racism are the following:

American Civil Liberties Union (ACLU)
132 W. 43d St.
New York, NY 10036
Telephone: (212) 944-9800
Not affiliated with any particular ethnic group, the ACLU works to counter governmental abuses that violate the civil rights and liberties of all citizens.

Anti-Defamation League of B'nai B'rith (ADL)
823 United Nations Plaza
New York, NY 10017
Telephone: (212) 490-2525

271

Fax: (212) 867-0779
Formed in 1913 to battle anti-Semitism in the United States, the ADL's mission has expanded to confront bigotry and racism of all forms.

National Association for the Advancement of Colored People (NAACP)
4805 Mt. Hope Dr.
Baltimore, MD 21215
Telephone: (410) 358-8900
Fax: (410) 486-9257
Founded in 1909, this organization is one of the oldest civil rights organizations in America. The NAACP has been influential in campaigns concerning voting rights, desegregation, job discrimination, and civil rights. The organization is open to people of all ethnic groups.

Other Organizations Working to End Racism

Center for Constitutional Rights
(formerly the Civil Rights Legal Defense Fund)
666 Broadway, 7th Floor
New York, NY 10012
Telephone: (212) 614-6464
Fax: (212) 614-6499

Congress of Racial Equity (CORE)
30 Cooper Square
New York, NY 10003
Telephone: (212) 598-4000
Fax: (212) 982-0184

People for the American Way
2000 M St., NW
Suite 400
Washington, DC 20036
Telephone: (202) 467-4999
Fax: (202) 293-2672

See Action 114 to learn more.

Southern Christian Leadership Conference (SCLC)
334 Auburn Ave., NE
Atlanta, GA 30312
Telephone: (404) 522-1420
Fax: (404) 659-7390

Action 113

Overcoming Environmental Racism

Despite the recent attempts by federal agencies to reduce environmental and health threats in the United States, inequities persist. If a community is poor or inhabited largely by people of color, there is a good chance that it receives less protection than a community that is affluent or white.

The geographic distribution of both minorities and the poor has been found to be highly correlated to the distribution of air pollution; municipal landfills and incinerators; abandoned toxic waste dumps; lead poisoning in children; and contaminated fish consumption. Virtually all studies of exposure to outdoor air pollution have found significant differences in exposure by income and race. Communities with hazardous waste incinerators generally have large minority populations, low incomes, and low property values; and penalties applied under hazardous waste laws at sites having the greatest white population were 500 percent higher than penalties at sites with the greatest minority population.

Environmental justice advocates have, in some cases, successfully sought to persuade federal, state, and local governments to adopt policies that address distributive impacts, concentration, enforcement, and compliance concerns. Some states have tried to use a "fair share" approach to come closer to geographic equity. In 1990, New York City adopted a fair legislative model designed to ensure that every borough and every community within each borough bears its fair share of noxious facilities. In 1994, President Clinton signed an executive order entitled

"Federal Actions to Address Environmental Justice in Minority Populations and Low-Income Populations,"which prohibits discriminatory practices in programs receiving federal financial assistance.*

What You Can Do

1. What's bad for any community is ultimately bad for all of us. Polluted air and contaminated groundwater know no geopolitical borders or socioeconomic boundaries. To help stem the problem, write to your local, state, and federal representatives to demand protection for communities of color. The following groups can give you plenty of information and suggestions on whom to contact.

Center for Ecology and Social Justice
c/o Institute for Policy Studies
1601 Connecticut Ave., NW
Suite 500
Washington, DC 20009
(202) 234-9382, ext. 240
The center supports the organizing and educational efforts of national and grassroots movements for environmental justice by strengthening collaboration between environmental justice organizations and cultural activists committed to progressive social change.

Citizen Action
1120 19th St., NW
Suite 630
Washington, DC 20036
(202) 466-3980

*Robert D. Bullard, "Overcoming Racism in Environmental Decision-making," *Environment*, May 1994. Reprinted with permission of the Helen Dwight Reid Educational Foundation. Published by Heldref Publications, 1319 18th St., NW, Washington DC 20036-1802. Copyright © 1994.

Citizen Action's toxics program focuses on preventing industrial pollution and on pesticides and food safety. The group issues annual national and state reports and supports legislative initiatives that promote environmental justice.

Citizen Alert
P.O. Box 5339
Reno, NV 89513
(702) 827-4200
Citizen Alert addresses national nuclear, military, and environmental issues from the perspective of how these impact on the people, land, and economy of Nevada and the Great Basin. The group has staffed programs on issues concerning nuclear waste, nuclear testing, toxics, water, and Native American sovereignty.

Citizen's Clearinghouse for Hazardous Wastes (CCHW)
P.O. Box 6806
Falls Church, VA 22040
(703) 237-2249
CCHW is a nationwide organization providing comprehensive assistance to local activists fighting hazardous wastes in their communities. Regional staff provides direct assistance, on-site organizing, and technical analysis. In addition CCHW disseminates information and grants for community leadership development.

The EcoJustice Network
A project of EcoNet (see Action 31), this is a great way to get involved if you have a computer.

Environmental Protection Agency
In response to President Clinton's Executive Order on Environmental Justice, the EPA has created an Office of Environmental Justice. Each of the EPA's ten regional offices has specific environmental justice programs and initiatives. For more information about regional offices, national initiatives, and publications, contact the Office of Environmental Justice, 401 M St., SW, Washington, DC 20460; (800) 962-6215 or (202) 260-6357.

Action 114

People for the American Way

It set a new standard of scrutiny for Supreme Court nominees in its successful effort to defeat Robert Bork. It has fought state-by-state battles to defend reproductive freedom. Without its support of the 1991 Civil Rights Act, many Americans would be at far greater risk of facing discrimination. People for the American Way's STAR program enlists and trains college students to lead discussions about diversity with over 23,000 middle and high school students.

Its action fund is perhaps better equipped and more effective at challenging and combating the dangerous influence of the Radical Right, including groups like Pat Robertson's Christian Coalition. As censorship in our schools soars, with attacks on classics like *Of Mice and Men,* and with sex education programs under fire, we can all feel just a bit more secure about the future of American education knowing that People for the American way is working day and night to protect free expression. The list of its contributions to improving respect for diversity; to protecting freedom of thought, expression, and religion; to fighting for equal justice; and to building a sense of community is perhaps unparalleled by any other group in this country.

What You Can Do

To help support its work, you can participate in phone banks, write letters to the editor, visit with your elected representatives, organize in your community, and assist local activities to monitor the Radical Right. For more information or to send a contribution, contact:

People for the American Way
2000 M St., NW
Suite 400

Washington, DC 20036
202-467-4999

Action 115

Women's Rights

After a decade of backlash, feminism is once again on the rise, and across the country, women are working for a platform that includes reproductive freedom, pay equity, a gender-balanced federal government, and equal-opportunity health care for women. For survivors of the '70's, this may sound like the same old song. But that's only because so many of the Steinem-era goals remain unachieved. In the United States for example, a woman is beaten by her spouse or boyfriend every 15 seconds; more than one third of American women live in counties without abortion providers; and two thirds of this country's minimum-wage workers are women. The grim statistics go on and on.

As befits an era in which the sound bite dominates national political discourse, the new feminism is strategically different from the women's rights movements of previous generations. Feminism's current wave takes to the streets with an immediacy designed to get not only attention but also fast results.*

A Guide to Women's Direct-Action Groups

WAC (Women's Action Coalition)

WAC was founded as a direct result of the Clarence Thomas/Anita Hill hearings. The group has clearly struck a chord with women across the country: WAC now claims roughly 2000 members in the New York metropolitan area and has branches in more than 20 cities, as well as fledg-

---

*Excerpted with permission from Mimi Udovitch, "Women in Action," *Harper's Bazaar*, Nov. 1992.

ling chapters in Paris and London. WAC meetings have acquired a certain cachet, conferred, in part, by the celebrities who often participate—Madonna came to one meeting, and performance artists Laurie Anderson and Holly Hughes are among the regular members.

WAC's strategic, high-energy actions ("WAC Attacks") are issue-oriented and media savvy. On Mother's Day, for example, WAC staged a protest at Grand Central Station with hundreds of participants, a drum corps, and banners that read: $30 BILLION OWED MOTHERS IN CHILD SUPPORT.

WHAM! (Women's Health Action and Mobilization)

Considered one of the more radical wings of the new feminist movement, WHAM! was founded three years ago in reaction to the Webster decision, the 1989 Supreme Court ruling that upheld a restrictive Missouri abortion law. Consequently, women's health—broadly interpreted here to include all forms of physical, mental, and economic health—is high on WHAM!'s agenda.

WHAM! is perhaps best known for its tireless defense of abortion clinics and its head-on confrontations with the strident antiabortion group Operation Rescue. Committed to educating women about their legal right to abortion, WHAM! has proved that it will mobilize in great numbers whenever those rights are compromised.

The Third Wave

In January of 1994, Rebecca Walker, the 22-year-old daughter of writer Alice Walker and goddaughter of Gloria Steinem, wrote an article in *Ms.* magazine outlining the need for a "third wave" of feminism. There were signs that many others felt the same way: The essay sparked some 100 supportive letters, all indignant at the steady erosion of women's rights. Soon after, Walker, along with Shannon Liss, founded the Third Wave, which they conceived of as a network to "utilize the energy" of young women across the country.

Convinced that their generation doesn't relate to such

established groups as the National Organization for Women (NOW), Walker and Liss founded the Third Wave as a more up-to-date alternative. They envision their organization as a broad-based, multicultural effort dedicated to fighting racism and environmental damage, as well as defending reproductive rights. To this end, they are sponsored by, among others, the Ms. Foundation and the National Black Women's Health Project.

For the most part, Third Wavers believe that the best way to change the system is by working with it, not against it. Says Liss, 'We want to pull the mainstream towards us, and the way to get our messages across is through magazines, TV, video, and advertising.'*

What You Can Do

Get involved with an organization that's focused on women's issues. Below is a list of just some of the many organizations that exist. It is not meant to be exhaustive, only to provide you with an idea about the different types of organizations you are likely to find.

American Civil Liberties Union
Women's Rights Project
132 W. 43d St.
New York, NY 10036
(212) 944-9800

Domestic Abuse Awareness Project (DAAP)
P.O. Box 1155
Madison Square Station
New York, NY 10159-1155
(212) 353-1755

*Excerpted with permission from Amruta Slee, "A Guide to Women's Direct-Action Groups," *Harper's Bazaar,* Nov. 1992.

Equal Rights Advocates (ERA)
1663 Mission St.
Suite 550
San Francisco, CA 94103
(415) 621-0672

Fund for the Feminist Majority
1600 Wilson Blvd.
Suite 801
Arlington, VA 22209
(703) 522-2214

National Organization for Women (NOW)
1000 16th St., NW
Suite 700
Washington, DC 20036
(202) 331-0066

National Women's Political Caucus
1275 K St., NW
Suite 750
Washington, DC 20005
(202) 898-1100

Religious Coalition for Reproductive Choice
1025 Vermont Ave., NW
Suite 1130
Washington, DC 20005
Telephone: (202) 628-7700
Fax: (202) 628-7716

Third Wave
185 Franklin St., 3d Floor
New York, NY 10013
(212) 925-3400

Women Express, Inc.
P.O. Box 6009 JFK

Boston, MA 02114

(617) 350-5030

Women Express, Inc., publishes Teen Voices *magazine, the only national forum that provides teenage girls a healthy, positive place to be published and to learn about resources and one another.*

Women's Action Coalition (WAC)

P.O. Box 1862

Chelsea Station, NY 10113

(212) 967-7711, ext. 9226

Women's Health Action Mobilization (WHAM)

P.O. Box 733

New York, NY 10009

(212) 560-7177

Women's Legal Defense Fund

1875 Connecticut Ave., NW

Suite 710

Washington, DC 20009

(202) 986-2600

2. Subscribe to magazines that publish women's works. This both supports women writers and provides you with insightful articles about women's issues and perspectives.

Action 116

Gay Rights

As with all forms of prejudice and discrimination, biases against gays and lesbians are based on fear and ignorance. Homosexuality is not a disease or a mental health problem. More than simply a lifestyle choice, it is a way of being which may be influenced by genetics and environmental factors. Like people everywhere, gays and lesbians are concerned with issues of family, livelihood, health care, education, retirement, and so on. The vast majority of people, through their lack of understanding, harbor dangerous misconceptions about gays that are often supported by social and governmental institutions. Consequently, gays and lesbian are also forced to deal with issues of securing their equal rights, protecting their safety, and raising awareness.

Education and other awareness-raising efforts have paid off the past few years, with a string of successes:

1. Israel joined Denmark, France, Norway, Sweden, Australia, the United States, and some Canadian provinces in outlawing discrimination in housing and employment based on sexual orientation.
2. After thirty-eight years on the books, a federal law prohibiting gay and lesbian foreigners from entering the United States has been repealed by Congress.
3. San Francisco voters approved a "domestic partners" referendum (extending benefits to nonmarried partners of city employees—a piece of legislation that dramatically affects gay and lesbian couples) and elected two openly lesbian women to the Board of Supervisors.
4. Denmark, Norway, and Sweden now recognize same-sex unions, making these the first countries in the world to grant nearly full legal rights to gays, lesbians, and bisexuals.

Sadly, amid the triumphs are also some sobering realities. For example, during 1993 there were 587 reported hate crimes against gays and lesbians in New York City alone. The Clinton administration's inability to institute its promised repeal of laws excluding gays from the military resulted in the sham policy of "don't ask, don't tell." Antigay initiatives are on the ballots in several states and local areas. Without greater awareness and understanding, it is likely that legislation similar to Colorado's ban on laws that would grant gays special consideration, such as protection from discrimination, may pass in other states.

What You Can Do

1. Just as with racism and sexism, the key to change starts with self-awareness. Whether you are straight or gay, there's probably much you can do to inform yourself and others around you about the need for greater understanding.
2. Support legislation that protects the rights of gays and lesbians.
3. Contact any of these organizations for more information:

Astraea Foundation
666 Broadway
Suite 510
New York, NY 10012
(212) 529-8021

Lambda Legal Defense and Education Fund
666 Broadway, 12th Floor
New York, NY 10012
Telephone: (212) 995-8585
Fax: (212) 995-2306

National Federation of Parents and Friends of Gays
8020 Eastern Ave., NW
Washington, DC 20012
(202) 726-3223

National Gay and Lesbian Task Force (NGLTF)
1734 14th St., NW
Washington, DC 20009
Telephone: (202) 332-6483

New York Lesbian and Gay Anti-Violence Project
647 Hudson St.
New York, NY 10014
(212) 807-6761

This organization has an excellent manual available for people who want to organize antiviolence projects.

Parents' Families and Friends of Lesbians and Gays
(PFLAG)
1012 14th St., NW
Suite 700
Washington, DC 20005
(202) 638-4200